# ROBERT SERVICE

## A BIOGRAPHY

Robert W. Service          *Blower Historical Collection, Edmonton*

# ROBERT SERVICE

## A BIOGRAPHY BY
## CARL F. KLINCK

DODD, MEAD & COMPANY
New York

**ROBERT SERVICE: A BIOGRAPHY**

Copyright © Carl F. Klinck, 1976.

Printed and bound in Canada

The publishers are grateful to the estate of Robert Service for permission to reproduce excerpts from the works of Robert Service in this book.

Library of Congress Cataloging in Publication Data

Klinck, Carl Frederick, 1908-
  Robert Service.

Bibliography: p.
1. Service, Robert William, 1874-1958—Biography.

PR6037.E72Z73          811'.5'2 [B]          76-22607
ISBN 0-396-07391-3

# Preface

This is the first biography of Robert W. Service (1874-1958), poet of the Gold Rush in the Canadian Yukon, and author of such well-known ballads as "The Shooting of Dan McGrew" and "The Cremation of Sam McGee." The full shelf of his works includes not only *Songs of a Sourdough* (*The Spell of the Yukon*), *Ballads of a Cheechako*, *Rhymes of a Rolling Stone*, and *Rhymes of a Red Cross Man*, but also nine other books of verse, three "collected volumes," six novels, and two autobiographies.

Late in his life, Service declared that all he wanted to be known of his "life story" was contained in *Ploughman of the Moon* (1945) and *Harper of Heaven* (1948). These two books, and *Why Not Grow Young? or Living For Longevity* (1928), were so written as to protect his privacy while his verses remained household words in Canada, the United States, and the United Kingdom.

This biography has been designed to find Service the man by combining evidence in these autobiographies, and other documents, with that which is subjective or subliminal in his novels, ballads, and songs. In his novels, for example, the principal characters are often masks for something in Service himself. And his dramatic ballads and songs abound in revelations of his literary program and the wisdom, humour, and compassion by which he lived.

The ballads which brought him fame and fortune were often an embarrassment for him, and he was indeed responsible for a deliberate choice of a public image as a gold-seeker, a Red Cross man, and, to the end of his life, a rough "old codger." Yet he declared with justice that he was "not his type." He was sympathetic to "rolling stones" but he was one of them in a very special way—a romantic adventurer and a realistic observer liberated (by wealth) to take the open road of his own choice and free (because of success) to write as he pleased.

His course was set in the Yukon, but his experiences brought many other romantic topics into his literary domain. He gave the "Gold Rush" treatment to stories or poems of the soldiers of the first World War, the Latin Quarter and the slums of Paris, the exotic scenery of Tahiti, the movie-land of Hollywood, the casinos of the Riviera, some international criminals, and the cities of Soviet Russia visited just before his remarkable escape from the German invaders of France.

This treatment was designed to do more than cater to the reader's curiosity, for Service was consistently dramatizing the give-and-take of joy and sorrow in the lives of "common" people. Few poets have produced a larger gallery of individualized characters in action than he sketched in his dramatic ballads and songs; and behind each character is his sense of the complexity, mystery, joy, and value of human life.

# Contents

1    Ayrshire and Glasgow      1
2    The Nemesis of Toil      17
3    The Yukon, Song and Story      31
4    Farewell to the North      59
5    The Literary World      77
6    Parisian Idyll, the Great      103
     War, and Hollywood
7    Tales of Evil in Paradise      135
8    New Adventures      153
9    Songs in Autumn      171
     Notes      193
     Books by Robert Service      198

# 1 Ayrshire and Glasgow

A few poems, "The Shooting of Dan McGrew" and "The Cremation of Sam McGee," have kept the reputation of Robert W. Service alive for readers and non-readers throughout the English-speaking world. Collections of his verse have therefore had a steady and profitable sale in bookstores since 1907, and the demand is now increasing because of the oil and tourist boom in Alaska and the Yukon.

Yet Service's autobiographies, *Ploughman of the Moon* and *Harper of Heaven,* have been out of print for several decades, and his six novels are little known, with the exception of one title, and only the title, of *The Trail of Ninety-Eight.* In biographical sketches, Service the man is lost in details about the Gold Rush, and information about his early and later life is usually missing. The popular assumption that he flourished and faded out as one of the "Dan McGrews" and "Sam McGees" is almost inevitable, although it is false.

The truth is that his personality and his way of

1

life were quite different from those of the characters whom he observed and described. The "I" and "me" in his stories and lyrics constituted a conventional literary device, a means of giving his observations a close impression of reality and, at the same time, providing a mask behind which he could preserve his privacy as a courteous and gentle soul.

A comprehensive view of his life and work is needed to reveal this otherwise unknown man, and such understanding can be opened to anyone who is willing to concede to this rhymer a poetic stance and purpose. The aura of romance and adventure is not lost in such an approach, for it will be found around his own life as well as around his verse. The private man who was Service himself exceeds in genuine human interest any character that he created for the public, for it had consistency and depth while the world of his observation and description left a fragmented impression of shifting fashions.

From his boyhood days, Service consciously built his outer world around an inner one in a way which amounted to a program. He saw things around him with a keen eye and stored them in his memory; his later travels were deliberately planned to increase this stock. All this time, through reading and uninhibited dreaming, he developed a habit of turning everything into romantic meanings and images which had the practical effect of selling his books and allowed him to live a life more adventurous than that of most other men.

This was not a process of self-delusion: he was well aware of what he was doing. By selling rhymes and stories made of his dreams, he won several fortunes which enabled him to turn many of his dreams into actual experiences of luxurious leisure, romance, and adventure, thus achieving what

many men can reach only in dreams. Along the line
where reality and fancy face one another, he made
a life for himself.

An obvious illustration of Service's coopera-
tion with his destiny appears in the fact that this im-
migrant from Scotland somehow managed to be in
Dawson City as a bank clerk in time to record one
of the most spectacular events in Canada's history.
His presence there was something more than a
piece of good luck. Seeing things as he did, he was
prepared to be where reality had become romance.

Service's boyhood was spent in Scotland, the
nurse of descriptive romancers like Walter Scott
and Robert Louis Stevenson who had found glamour where many people had seen only hard facts.
The reality Service experienced in early life is set
forth in *Ploughman of the Moon*; the dream-coloured
fiction is in *The Trail of Ninety-Eight*.[1] Athol Meldrum, the narrator of that novel, resembles Service
in certain ways: in the "Prelude", Meldrum, now an
old man back in Scotland reminiscing about the
Gold Rush, pictures his boyhood home as an ances-
tral estate where "a great peat fire" is lighting

> *the oak-panelled hall; the crossed*
> *claymores gleam, the eyes in the*
> *mounted deer-heads shine glassily;*
> *rugs of fur cover the polished floor.*

It was the home of a laird in Glengyle, in the West
Highlands, where "the Scotch mist [is] silvering the
heather and the wind [is] blowing caller from the
sea." Meldrum is now a laird.

This was fable, but there is something of Service's boyhood in it. Robert had lived on the edge
of the West Highlands and his Aunt Jeannie had
tried to make a hardy "Hielandman" of him by in-

sisting on his wearing of the kilts. He had certainly
not lived with the rank and luxury of Athol Meldrum, and he had not been the brother and successor to a laird. He was, however, a literary heir of
Scott's and Stevenson's romantic characters, as any
Scottish lad dares to be. And while he was writing
*The Trail of Ninety-Eight* in 1910, he was surviving
the Gold Rush with less pain than Meldrum, and
he was achieving an income which even a laird
might envy.

It is characteristic of Service that there were
always traces of personal experience in his romances. It would be folly to assert that Athol Meldrum mirrored the author of *The Trail of Ninety-
Eight* in most respects, but something vital to a
biography would be lost if Service's descriptions of
the boy Athol were passed over as entirely fictitious. Who, indeed, was this boy, "roaming the wild
heather hills," who "heard the glad shouts of the
football players on the green, yet never ettled to
join them"? And is it inappropriate to see Robert in
the Athol of those days, "a little shy-mannered lad
in kilts, bare-headed to the hill breezes, with
health-bright cheeks, and a soul happed up in
dreams," who "lived in an enchanted land, a land
of griffins and kelpies, of princesses and gleaming
knights"? "It was a wonderful gift of visioning that
was mine in those days," Robert's Athol continues:
"it was the bird-like flight of the pure child-mind to
whom the unreal is yet the real."

Robert followed "the banner" of his boyish
kind of romance, not in Athol's "West Highlands,"
but in the West Lowlands and in Glasgow, Gateway
to the Isles. He had been transported to Scotland
when he was a very young child. The earliest days
in England went unremembered by the child and
the man who, late in his life, would dilute the

straight Scotch of *Ploughman of the Moon* with only a few drops of reference to that other part of Britain.

His father, Robert Service, was a Scot; his mother (Emily, née Parker) was English. They were living at 4 Christian Road[2], in Preston, Lancashire, when Robert was born on January 16th, 1874. "Papa" gave up his employment in a bank when "Mama" inherited ten thousand pounds from her father, "who owned cotton mills." They belonged to a class which Robert described as "middle-middle". After the family moved back to Glasgow, "Papa's" native city, the family grew to a total of seven boys and three girls.[3]

When that move was made, young Robert, the eldest, was sent to live with his grandfather Service and three maiden aunts in Ayrshire. Although the "Long Grey Town" of his childhood is not named in *Ploughman of the Moon,* it is described as consisting of a single street of whin-grey houses, where there were neighbouring coalpits, iron works, a castle, and an abbey. Such evidence pointed to Kilwinning, which had Eglinton Castle in a spacious park, the ruins of the Monastery of St. Winning, and the remains of the Eglinton Iron Works. Confirmation has been found in the Rev. William Lee Kerr's *Kilwinning* (1900), kindly supplied by Miss Jane G. McMillan, the Senior Assistant Librarian of the Ayr County Library. In this book appears this statement:[4]

> *Mr. John Service was appointed postmaster in 1861, he had a small office, and a postman to help him in his duties. Since that time, and especially since the present postmistress, Miss Janet Service, was appointed in 1887, changes have been rapid and the work of the office marvellously increased.*

*Germaine Service*

Robert Service at about two years of age.

As Robert reported it: "Grandfather was postmaster; Aunt Bella sold stamps, while Aunt Jennie jiggled a handle that in some inconceivable way sent off telegrams. Aunt Jeannie ran the house," he added, "and looked after the garden and the hens,"—and looked after young Robert. A fourth aunt, "puir Aggie," had died of consumption.[5] In their old-fashioned house the family practised an unemotional moral discipline, and kept the Scotch Sabbath with church-going at the Auld Kirk in a strict routine which was "misery" to the freedom-loving boy, who developed a life-long distaste for religious services.

Being a lonely child in this household, Robert exhibited a juvenile tendency to be a "show-off," hiding courageously the fact that he was really imaginative, nervous, and shy. Stories and rhymes began to fascinate him. He took a "gruesome delight" in one of the family's few approved volumes, Foxe's *Book of Martyrs*. While attending the parish school at the age of five or six, he discovered his "story-telling gift" and his facility in rhyming. The tales were all "make-believe," what he would later call "dream-stuff." Significantly, he recognized one of the prerequisites of literary work: "the unreal is yet the real" if the craftsmanship is adequate. "I never believed in fairy tales," he recorded in *Ploughman of the Moon*, "but I could make others do so." His first public exhibition of versifying was a risky affair of making up his own grace at table:

> God bless the cakes and bless the jam
> Bless the cheese and the cold boiled ham
> Bless the scones Aunt Jennie makes
> And save us all from belly-aches.
>
> > Amen.

Everything was grist to his mill, even church

and Sunday School. The "likeable tunes" of the hymns were something to enjoy. "Indeed, in later years," he said, "I slightly altered some of the melodies and turned them into comic songs."

Such liberties were forgiven by his aunts because Robbie Burns had set a precedent. After all, this was the land of Burns, for Kilwinning was not far from Kilmarnock, Mossgiel, and Ayr. Burns was in the family tradition. "My great-grandfather," Service wrote later, "had been a crony of Robert Burns and claimed him as a second cousin. One of our parlour chairs had often been warmed by the rump of the Bard. . . . To my folks anything that rhymed was poetry, and Robbie Burns was their idol." For the young boy in the house, Burns was "tops" as poet; Robert felt a "spiritual kinship" with the freedom-loving ploughman who evoked respect for earthiness in this precocious "ploughman of the moon." The boy "preferred humour to sentiment and liked it racy," and developed "an urge to shock people."

As early as this, the boy had evidently become acquainted with Shakespeare, for he tried to persuade his friend Pat that his Ayrshire favourite was "greater" than the Stratford master. Pat liked "the Anglicized verse," while young Robert "preferred the Doric . . . the tongue of our town and every word was vital." Whether in romance or in homely reality Robert could, as Athol Meldrum said of himself, "glory in details."

The Ayrshire period came to an end when, on the occasion of a visit by Robert's father and mother (who had come down from Glasgow), Aunt Jeannie insisted that the boy wear his "Hielandman" finery. His mother discovered that he had "*nothing on* under his kilts," and was further appalled by Jeannie's broad joke about the advantages thereof. Robert was "retrieved" and taken to Glasgow to live, at first in lonely embarrassment, with "a swarm of brothers."

Their home in Glasgow was number 19 in "a four-storey block of flats called Roselea Terrace," on a street now known as Roxburgh. Opposite it was a similar block called Ferndale Terrace. Both were "grim and gloomy," and "only in summer did the sunshine gild [their] door-mat." "But," he added, "it was a highly respectable street, where we lived in genteel poverty"—a "front of *bourgeois* respectability." Robert attended Church Street Primary School at the foot of Byers Road,[6] which he described as "a plebeian board-school," a "drab school," "in a dubious region between slumland and respectability," where there were games and gang fights.

By his own confession he was an impertinent and exhibitionist boy whose chief literary concern was the reading of romantic stories by Manville Fenn and Talbot Baines Reed. Jimmy, one of his friends, drew caricatures and read some novels, the approved *Boys' Own Paper*, and improving articles such as *How to Stuff Birds*, but he failed to raise Robert's standards. (Jimmy became James Bone, a distinguished journalist, appointed editor of the *Manchester Guardian* in 1912.)[7]

On the 3rd of August, 1885, Robert was enrolled in a brand new school, Hillhead, opened as a "Public School" in April of that year. A booklet entitled *Hillhead High School 1885-1961*[8] gives an account of this "dream" institution, reputed to be "the Finest School in Scotland," which was only five minutes from Roselea Terrace. The Headmaster was Edward Ellice Macdonald, who stressed academic learning; but, as the booklet states, "he was still more intent on making it a building-place of character, a training-ground for his pupils to fit themselves for the duties, responsibilities, and privileges of citizenship." After the first nine years, Macdonald saw Hillhead recognized locally as a Secondary, or High, School. At that time the enrolment had grown to nine hundred.

Robert attended Hillhead from 1885 until 1888, from his eleventh until his fourteenth year. He was a rather indifferent student (except in English literature), who enjoyed bullying the masters. At the age of fourteen, he was expelled "with kid gloves" for his "defiance of the drill-master," evidently an old soldier named William Walker. He had not cared much for games: the only time he distinguished himself in school football was when he split his shorts on the field.

His habit of living a double life of realism and romance grew stronger, for it was destined to remain with him until the end. Romance, however, acquired a new definition, as it did for Athol Meldrum, the narrator of *The Trail of Ninety-Eight*, who recorded his sudden arrival "at a second phase of [his] mental growth in which fancy usurped the place of imagination." The modern equivalents of Romance attracted me," Athol added, "and with my increasing grasp of reality, my gift of vision faded."

Robert's progress was not made in school so much as in Miss Bell's Circulating Library ("a penny for a book") and the Public Library ("a city of books," three miles from home). He was a "ravenous reader." "Between ten and twenty," he records, "I did the bulk of my life-reading." In the first three of those years he "pursued [his] adventures in the fiction of the day" (Athol's "modern equivalents"). "It was exciting enough," Service ex-

plained in *Ploughman,* "Stevenson, Rider Haggard,
James Reid, Besant and Rice—all held me spell-
bound." These, and *Punch.*

Robert was "close to thirteen" when he spent
three glorious months by the sea. After this "wonderful summer" he regarded a seaman's life in
both realistic and romantic ways. He "spent every
Saturday wandering the docks," and regretted
later that he had not been able to go on the ships
"to get a good sea-ground for a writer." His fancy
first played around a sailor's deportment on
shore—the swaggering "in brass buttons and grow-
[ing] tough and strong." Characteristically he
added, "How I would come back with weird stories
of wild lands!" Athol Meldrum also recorded the
transition from dreams "of knights-errants, of cor-
sairs and of outlaws" to dreams of contemporary
adventure whose realities a fortunate young man
might go forth to experience.

Robert's parents thought otherwise. At the age
of fourteen he made a "false start" in the drudgery
of a newly established and unsuccessful shipping
office—the next best thing to going to sea. He did
not like such work. When he was fifteen, he decided, to his father's delight, upon a change to the
more congenial employment of an apprentice in a
bank—the Stobcross branch of the Commercial
Bank of Scotland.[9] Here he stayed six years, (1889
until 1896), while he continued his reading and ex-
perimented with writing for publication.

He began with poetry. Tennyson's "Ulysses"
and Browning's "A Toccata of Galuppi's" marked
"the peak of [his] appreciation." "But it was to
minor bards," such as Owen Meredith and Coven-
try Patmore, that he "turned for real enjoyment."
"Even more," he said, he liked "verse-makers" as

models—Thackeray, Hood, Poe—"with lots of rhyming." No reader needs to be told that he "was always in love with rhyme":

> *If two lines could be made to clink it seemed to me to go a long way to justify them. Perhaps it was because I had such facility in that direction . . . while at home, I often spoke in stanzas. Rhyming has my ruin been. With less deftness I might have produced real poetry.*

Experimentation led to modest success as a contributor to Glasgow periodicals. "The Song of Social Failure" appeared in the *Herald*, "It Must Be Done" in *Scottish Nights,* and "Shun Not the Strife" in the *People's Friend*—altogether over a score of poems in the local weeklies. He wrote during office hours or while he was walking "through the lovely park, lingering in pleasant places dreaming and reciting." Sentiment reigned while he thought he was in love with Maisie McQuarrie, "the perfection of prettiness." He was too shy to cope with her and her "snooty" parents, but he poured out his affection for her in "Love's Lament", which offered these lines:

> *Love's exultant roundelay*
> *Issues in a wail of pain.*

("I was so tickled with it" he said later, "that, being Scotch, I saved it up and used it on three later occasions under somewhat similar but less reticent circumstances.") He lacked experience: "I talked of books instead of her looks. I gave her Keats when she wanted cuddling."[10]

Although he laboriously "aped Keats for sonnets and Austin Dobson for ballades," he soon grew sick of "nectar," that is, of poetical words and subject matter "such as mythology and nature," and concern with beauty, form, "ideals and abstractions." He felt the greater attraction of what he called "beer", Anglo-Saxon words, themes of ugliness, vice, "eating and drinking, and lusts and common people." He exploited the rhythmic patterns of newspaper verse, "neat but negligible," usually on "the three verse pattern—attack, build-up and pay-off." Bret Harte and Eugene Field became models for him just before he said farewell to poetry about the age of seventeen, and took up games. Under the coaching of friendly MacSporran, and equipped with a special pair of boots loaded with some lead, he had a successful season as the kicking fullback on a rugger team and actually made a long run over touch. In the next season he did quite well as a cricketer: he "willed" the batsmen to put the ball where he could catch it. His batting average was "two not out, as [he] went in last man." His enthusiasm for sports lasted only one year.

Tiring of athletics, Service frequented the music halls and educated himself in pubs and in vaudeville. "Its rum-tum, rumtittytum inspired some of [his verses]," he confided to his autobiography, "and when [he] played at song composing it was in the tempo of the old-fashioned musichall." It is intriguing to remember how much, but how differently, the American, Walt Whitman, had been inspired in the atmosphere of Italian opera.

For Service, the natural consequence was to step up and become a devotee of the theatre, where Glasgow afforded attendance at performances by professional actors such as Henry Irving, Ellen Terry, Wyndham and Willard, as well as "provincial players", such as J. T. Toole, Edward Terry, Edward Compton, and Osmond Tearle. Robert began to declaim Hamlet and Macbeth, and to study elocution in preparation for dramatic roles.

His success was meagre. He carried a banner in *Marmion*, played second watchman in *Macbeth*, and Robert, son of *Rob Roy*. His greatest success was accidental: he won applause when he inadvertently made a hurried appearance on stage with his kilt on backward.

These experiments with words suggest that Glasgow, and not primarily the hobo camps of the American Pacific coast, made Service's voice and ear adaptable to the free turns of speech in which this boy from the land of Burns characterized and immortalized the common, unbookish language of the Yukon. When the theatre "cast [him] out," Service visioned himself in cap and gown as a student of the university, which stood in "serene beauty" and dignity, "high soaring from the hill" above the park with its winding river, where he walked daily from Roselea Terrace to his work. He matriculated and became a part-time college student. He left after Christmas when he had received only twenty-three marks for a paper which he had valued at ninety; he had tried to suggest that Ophelia in *Hamlet* was "a bit of a slut."

He turned to a study of literature of a more congenial kind. Stevenson, Kipling, and Jack London inspired him, but the two writers who most influenced his life were Henry David Thoreau and George Borrow. *Walden* avoided the adornment of shallow books, and presented Service, in "simplicity of expression," with "a clean new world of tonic air and diamond clarity"; Thoreau "fostered the recluse," and perhaps the potential farmer in Service. *Lavengro* introduced him to "a great and original writer," "a fine, handsome man, a fighter and lover of horses, a friend of gypsies, a rover and a student"; Borrow revealed to Service "the gift of vagrancy"—"he was one of the unsettling urges that made "[the young bank clerk] a lover of the open road"; he "kindled the wanderlust."

Whether he knew it or not, Robert was being absorbed into current literary fashions of vagabondage and interest in low life. The next chapter in *Ploughman of the Moon,* is entitled "Proletarian Prig" and begins, "Back to dear old slumland [bordering the bank] with its dockers, its derelicts and its dreams." For a time, at the age of eighteen, he dallied, until he was bored, with radicalism, socialism, materialism, and rationalism.

Then came a "bohemian interlude" with a gay gang of Glasgow youths, among whom were some aspiring writers. Their leader was a talented young man named Mugson, who was doomed to die at a very early age. As a writer of whimsical, witty stories, he achieved some success with a serial in a weekly paper:[11]

> *It was called:* Tom, Dick and Harry, *and we were all in it. It was the forerunner of a school that was called the New Humour. Jerome, Barry Pain and Jacobs were its leading exponents, and the* Idler *and* To-day *its chief vehicles.*

Robert now read French literature: Zola, Flaubert, de Maupassant, and the de Goncourts—also Balzac and Hugo. George Moore's *Confessions of a Young Man* appealed to him, and living in a Paris garret became a goal, which had to be postponed because Morley Roberts' *Western Avernus* confirmed an alternative ambition to "go to America and become a hobo."

Since it was difficult to save money to enable him to become independent of work in the bank, Service was inspired, by a younger brother's enthusiasm for farm life in Fifeshire, to plan a "bucolic phase," in which he would grow as rugged as his conception of "a Highland Scot, clad in the tartan, high up on a misty mountain, with a pair of shaggy dogs and a herd of huge-horned cattle."

This description parallels the picture later drawn of Athol Meldrum and of Athol's brother Garry, who also figures in the plot of *The Trail of Ninety-Eight.* Like Athol, Robert merged dreams of farming with a prospective later period ending in vagabondage. Romance had taken this decisive turn; as Athol put it, "I now dreamed of cowboys, of gold-seekers, of beach-combers. . . . I read avidly all I could find dealing with the Far West." More practically, Athol's mother, remembering a cousin who had done well as a sheep-rancher in the Saskatchewan valley, sent her son to join the cousin in the Canadian Far West.

Service read all the pamphlets about Canada which he could obtain from the Emigration Office, and set his goal on becoming "a sturdy settler, raising cattle and grain, or riding a bronco and roping steers." The opportunity to make and save money for the trip abroad arrived in 1895 with Robert's transfer from the Stobcross branch to the St. Vincent Street branch of the bank, involving promotion to Junior Clerk and an increase in salary from twenty to seventy pounds per annum.[12]

Both narrator and novelist took leave of tearful mothers at the docks in Glasgow to sail to the New World. A month later, Athol was in San Francisco, not in Saskatchewan, for he had decided to be a hobo, gypsy, and beachcomber on Stevenson's "glamorous islands" for "a few thistledown years." Service, however, a "steerage emigrant" on a tramp steamer, travelled directly to a ranch on Vancouver Island, British Columbia, and postponed hoboing on the Pacific Coast of the United States until he had spent two years on a Canadian farm.

# 2 The Nemesis of Toil

Service's resignation from the bank of Glasgow took effect on the 31st of March, 1896.[1] It was spring, the season which he thought "would best give him a happy start to a life of hazard." He crossed the Atlantic as a steerage emigrant on a tramp steamer, and approached Canada by way of Newfoundland, the Gulf, and the St. Lawrence, with excitement and eager anticipation, being "poor and friendless," but envying no one "because [he] was young and in love with life."[2]

A "colonist" train took him across Canada to the Pacific coast. He must have been an amusing sight as he openly displayed the part of a gun-slinging cowboy which he had practised at home. In the toilet of the train, he changed into a Buffalo Bill costume which his father had bought for him in an auction room: "it consisted of a pair of high circus boots and a Spanish sombrero."

Adventure and freedom were his goals; he had "an aversion for strenuous forms of toil." So

17

the prairies distressed him; he felt that making a living there would be hard and unglamourous, "fit only for Swedes and Slovacs." Yet he wished to wander where he could do a modest amount of work with his hands. He had arrived in Canada with only five dollars in his pocket, and he had been obliged to sell his bags, his Harris tweed suit, his gun, his camera, and other articles to provide cash on his way across the continent. He kept on travelling as far as the trains would go—to the west coast of British Columbia—and then across the water to Vancouver Island.

Two months after his departure from Scotland, he had a job, not as a cowboy, but as a labourer on a farm near Duncan, north of the city of Victoria. His first tasks of picking up stones and sawing wood fell short of the picturesque activities which he had expected to find on Robert Louis Stevenson's trail of adventure. Stevenson had travelled to California by emigrant ship and train in 1879, when Robert Service was five years of age, and to the South Seas in 1888. Had the boy been brought up in England, he might have planned to follow Kipling to India or Australia. As fate would have it, he was lured by Canada, where there were "lots of Scots," and where he went with a copy of Stevenson's *An Amateur Emigrant* in his pocket.

He was not wholly unprepared for the labour which would be involved in travel, since, in Glasgow when he was nearly twenty, he had read Morley Roberts' *The Western Avernus,* subtitled "Toil and Travel in Further North America." This book "first kindled the spirit of vagabondage" in Service and inspired his characterization of himself as an itinerant worker and a durable, if suffering, hobo. Roberts' account opened in Texas with a reference to Bret Harte, from whom came his "notions of

Western America." In the course of the volume,
there are many descriptions of Roberts' travel and
work in Canada under such chapter headings as
"To Manitoba and the Rockies," "The Kicking
Horse Pass," "The Railroad Camps," "Round Kamloops," "Through the Fraser Canyon," "Down
Stream to the Coast," "New Westminster," and "To
Vancouver Island and Victoria." Roberts had
moved northwestward to Canada from the United
States and had ended these travels in San Francisco; Service was starting in Canada and dreaming
of the South.

In the meantime, he was employed on a Vancouver Island farm which belonged to a Shetland
family, whom he called the McTartans. He later
described his status as a "mud pupil" who enjoyed
haying because of the physical exercise, but who
hated milking. There was much in his environment
which he could romanticize; he saw himself as a pi-
oneer, growing more muscular every day, working
"in the green wonder of the primeval forest," "a
dream world worthy of a dreamer." His social position began its descent, for the life of the Old
Country emigrants was glorified by the Old School
Tie. Service was only more or less on "the snob-
side." When he lived through the winter with "Old
Hank," cultivating laziness in a nearby backwoods
ranch, he was reduced to "the mossbank section."
Brashly dramatizing this part with a black shirt, a
white tie, and a black stetson, he posed as a roughneck, dropping his English accent and practising
the use of the vernacular.

He soon learned that experience was going to
demand a heavy price, but for a time he clung to
the theories of his future with which, and for
which, he had come. He believed that he could accept the bad with the good. "Instinct told him that,

in throwing over the traces and staking his fate on the unknown, he was unconquerably right. . . ." With regard to romance and reality, he thought that he had the gift "to see the ordinary with the eyes of marvel." "It may be," he said, "there is no ordinary and wonder is true vision. In any case it keeps one spiritually intact." He would "live lyrically." His dreams would collaborate with his destiny. He "would never allow himself to be shaped by circumstances." Freedom to voyage where he willed would make his dreams come true. He had no fear of the future.

He believed that he could "create experience," so that he might be able to write about it. Roberts had done that. As the latter had got his material for *The Western Avernus,* Service would accumulate his own, perhaps for a book, "by self-sought adventures." "The thought," he recalled, "was always at the back of my mind. I might commit all kinds of folly, but my pen would save me in the end. It may have been that instinctive confidence that made me so jaunty and challengeful of fate."

As if by something more than chance, he found a pile of old *Harper's Magazines* in Hank's shack. These provided intellectual stimulation and fired all kinds of ambitions. His goal was San Francisco, but months of labour were needed for the acquisition of funds. In the spring of 1897, he left the farm and old Hank's backwoods place and became a "cow-juice jerker"—not a cowboy but at least a cowman, "a manipulator of manure," at the biggest ranch in the area. This appeared also to be "a false turning," but he enjoyed the summer work and the feeling that he could earn "his bread by the sweat of his brow." In November he left to spend the winter of 1897-1898 in the South.

In December he was in Seattle, where he

bought, for one dollar, a ticket for San Francisco
on a steamship called *Mariposa.* The accommoda-
tion was scarcely worth that price, and seasickness
made things worse. He was one of a hundred
hobos, or at least "half a hobo." He felt, neverthe-
less, "a sense of destiny." He had no misgivings. He
was beginning "to see a definite design in his future." Instead of waiting for adventure he would
go to meet it, and "the more colourful it was, the
more arresting would be his copy."

He spent a month in San Francisco, exploring
every bit of that city which had "most kindled his
imagination . . . Bret Harte, the Argonauts, the
gold rush." He meditated at the Memorial in the
Plaza dedicated to Robert Louis Stevenson, a "little
bronze galleon on its granite shaft," unveiled only a
month earlier. The theatres, the restaurants, the
joss-houses, the waterfront, the dives, the scum of
the Seven Seas fascinated him while his funds
melted away. "I was terribly alone," he remembered, "and though alone, I had no fear of the future. I might be down in the gutter, but I had faith
in my star." He was "becoming tough, using the
language of the roughneck, and behaving like
one." When only one ten-dollar bill remained, he
had his first feeling of fear. He had seen so much
"of the misery of a great city, its derelicts, its down-
and-outs that their degradation filled him with disgust." He was scared.

It was a turning point. When he answered an
advertisement for "labourers wanted for the Los
Angeles area," he was offered a job as "a handy-
man, half coachman, half gardener, for two old ladies" at twenty-five dollars a month. It was a position which promised a comfortable and settled
existence. He was, therefore, facing "one of those
cross-roads of destiny." Acceptance would have al-

tered his whole future, but he refused in order to follow his dream. Someone else "seemed to be speaking through [his] mouth as [he] said 'No.' " The job which he did take as a "tunneller" in the San Gabriel Canyon proved to be a "bit of hell," and he left as soon as he could, with a cheque to be cashed in Oakland. Needing the money, he sold it for half its value. He was rapidly reaching the lowest depths of a "human doormat," "just another bum to be treated like a dog," "a bit of flotsam to be spat on, scorned." Bitterly, he considered how to keep on going "forward to whatever destiny awaited him."

Such considerations gave Service's record of this trip, published forty years later in *Ploughman of the Moon*, levels of personal meaning deeper than one finds in Roberts' professional travel writing. Service was engaged in a desperate adventure of soul-searching.

On the afternoon of Christmas day, 1897, he arrived by train in Los Angeles, where he lived with bums in an evangelical mission. He sank into an easy life without "brute toil." But he had time to ask himself whether possessing his own soul in this condition was enough. Was he fitted for anything? He was heading for disaster, although his literary interests were revived. There was a delightful Public Library where "day after day [he] browsed on books of verse." He wanted to write "newspaper poetry, the kind that simple folks clip out and paste in scrap-books." Yet his dream was fading into a greater aloofness from the realities of life until semi-starvation and a sense of panic made him realize that he could not continue this shiftless existence. In the New Year he reached twenty-four years of age.

The very temporary "mindless" task of carrying an advertising banner inspired him to write a parody on "Excelsior," but this employment paid for only a few meals. A job as an orange picker near the city was pleasant, but it did not last very long.

He advertised in a local paper for a job requiring a certain amount of education. This brought him an offer of a position in San Diego as "a sort of tutor" to three girls who needed cultural conversation. At the "Villa Lilla", a mission-like building with a "monastic-looking door," set in a delightful garden in a suburb of San Diego, he found out that he was to be a substitute for an absent black man who had done odd jobs. He accepted, and rejoiced in the variety of his work around the place, which he discovered was a high-class brothel whose mysteries were guarded from him by Madame. The girls were attractive, but maintained a significant distance. When the black man's return was imminent, Service was sent away with a gift from one of the girls—a guitar with a brown leather case, the equipment of a troubadour.

This instrument was related in a special way to his past. He could not remember when he had not played some instrument. As a boy he had begun with a penny whistle. He had been given piano lessons at the age of nine. Then he had gone on to a flute, a piccolo, a concertina, a banjo, and, at Old Hank's among the Douglas firs, another banjo, a battered one to which he sang songs. Fate had now handed him an instrument with which he could become a wandering minstrel and continue his gypsy travels. He would not allow himself to be "broken on the wheel of toil." "Better than bondage," he thought, was "vagabondage." So, once more, he took the course of least resistance, tempting fate.

As he was near Mexico, he decided to visit that

country, but the novelty soon wore off and the nights were cold for a man with no roof over his head. Feelings of unreality often came over him now. "I was going forward," he recalled "in a dream in which I seemed to have lost all contact with the past." Romantic journeying had its bitter side. He had wasted his youth in foolish adventure, turning his back on society, and society might refuse to take him back. He drifted northwards towards Los Angeles—first to Santa Ana—feeling "suddenly forlorn." There was no place for him in this land. "Where was he driving to?"

Near Los Angeles, circumstances offered him a reprieve. A schoolboy, whose name turned out to be Jimmy Service, invited him to meet his "Pop." Robert took stock of his own appearance. The night before had been the worst in his experience as a hobo. He had been joined in his improvised hut of old railway ties by a stranger whom he presumed was the robber and killer known to be in that neighbourhood. Robert had crawled out of the shelter and had dozed in a hollow full of dried leaves. He now felt ashamed to be seen by the boy's Scottish family. Yet he had "a moment of hesitation." "I felt," he recalled, "it was one of the crossroads of destiny, in which my choice would make the greatest difference to my future. Here might be a chance to make good." The family might put him on his feet. His response was characteristic:

> *Then something seemed to twist me right round, and bidding [the boy] good-bye, I went off in the opposite direction. . . . What is directing my steps? . . . Well, a force stronger than myself seemed to be drawing me on to another destiny, and, even though it looked a gloomy one, I must fulfill it.*

Yet he had enough of a shock to consider the future he was risking. Discouraged, he sat in a public square in the outskirts of Los Angeles and thought about what he had become, one of "the Great Unwanted, incapable of hard work and unable to get soft jobs"—in short, an outcast, like those who would die in ditches. He had rugged health, but not the hands for heavy labour, or even for dishwashing. What he longed for was a white-collar job. The mere wish was a small step up, but little confidence in his ability remained. He dodged decisions by meditating: *"What will be must be. The future as well as the past is a fixation. To-day was conditioned by yesterday, and to-morrow will be conditioned by to-day. Life is a pattern, woven to the last thread. What I do is the only thing I can do."* He knew that this was dangerous doctrine: "The Law of Cause and Effect supreme in the Universe. Determinism to the last degree. Free will a mockery." His destiny he insisted, "was on the knees of the gods, and there was nothing [he] could do about it." Not quite nothing, however: he could always dream and invite the unfolding of the Pattern. Years later, in *Ploughman* (p. 354), he called this response to life "the romance of destiny."

Now began a series of events in which luck or coincidence played such a part that such fatalism seemed validated. Beside him a man had been reading a newspaper. He left it behind him: it told Service about the gold strike in the Klondike. He was not interested in what happened in a land colder than British Columbia. Paradoxically, however, the language caught his imagination, for the report went on to say that "no doubt another Bret Harte will arise and sing of it in colourful verse." Here was Service's destiny—by singing of the gold rush to make the richest strike of all—but not yet!

Only the words "arise and sing" stirred Service at this moment.

He arose to sing his way for many months of 1898 through Colorado, Nevada, Arizona: "over much of the West." By a piece of bad luck he lost his guitar on a long railway tressle in the Tehachapi Mountains. So fate made him decide to return toward the North. On the way, his attempt to work in a sawmill in Oregon ended in failure, and persuaded him again that "Nature intended him to be a dud." Another newspaper left on a bench caught his eye with a bit of news about British Columbia. He took a boat for Canada on his way to the big ranch on which he had worked near Duncan.

There he became once more a cowman, in charge of fifty cows and their calves. The work was hard, but he could handle it during the summer and autumn, with opportunities for independence and for private thought. Winter, however, began to double his responsibilities and in December, a big, black bull laid him low with cracked ribs. Even before this accident, he had doubted his ability to carry on through the winter; his future seemed hopeless: he might as well go back to being a tramp in the warm South. "I was desperate," he wrote. "The gods were laughing at my plight. Would they ever give me a break? . . . Utterly discouraged, I cursed the gods."

The whole course of his life changed as he lay nursing his ribs. His friend Bill, the storekeeper, quit his job, and Service was appointed his successor. Fate, or luck, had come unexpectedly to his rescue—at last he was "once again a white-collar man . . . a bourgeois"—eating with the boss's family, and at work enjoying a leisurely routine which allowed time for books and meditation. He went to parties, fished for salmon, and played in amateur theatricals, but he particularly valued the opportunities for reading novels borrowed from the local library. This was quite a change from the preceding years, when, as he said, "literature did not exist for him." But there "was no music and no verse" in him at this time.

The ranch was his home for four years, probably from early in 1899 until some time in 1903, while he was twenty-five to twenty-nine years of age. He later thought of these as stagnant years, a period of wasted time because it was an easy existence; in these "rubber-stamp days," living was not strenuous enough to be the life for which he had longed. He had few achievements as a salesman, except to sell chamber pots as Etruscan vases to Indian women, and he saw the store going down hill because he had no talent for competitive business. Once more, he was a square peg in a round hole. An old mossback advised him to try something else, perhaps schoolteaching.

That would be something beyond a mere white-collar! It would be a profession! He decided to go to school to prepare for his matriculation examination, and to work in the summer to bolster his initial bank balance of two hundred dollars. Living in a friend's shack he did some intense studying, and he tried to do more while tired out by summer work on the roads. The examination, evidently held in Vancouver or Victoria, brought him failures in math and French. But an interest in verse had been revived. He sent a sentimental poem of three stanzas, entitled "Apart and Together" to *Munsey's*. It was published two months later in the December 1903 issue of that magazine. This is what he had dreamed of doing. But facing a college course with a deficit of two supplementals was too much for his patience.

Once more he looked for a job. This time he assisted fate to make him a white-collar man by buying a new serge suit and an overcoat. No doubt he kept quiet about what he really wanted to be: "a ragtime kid in a honky-tonk, a rose gardener, a Parisian *apache,* a librarian, a rural delivery postman, a herring fisherman." He was turned down by a person requiring an office boy. But luck or fate was waiting on the street, its agent being a traveller for a biscuit firm, who suggested that Service should apply for a job as a clerk in the very bank before which they were standing. Clutching the testimonial from the manager of the Stobcross branch of the Bank of Scotland—a document he carried because it was his only certificate of recommendation—Service went into this Vancouver bank and was hired. On October 10th, 1903, he entered the employ of the Canadian Bank of Commerce at Victoria, British Columbia.[3]

The strange ways of fate made their impression upon Service. "On what accidents," he wrote, "do our destinies depend! What seeming trifles may change our entire lives! How we are at the mercy of the insignificant!" Reflections of this as a literary *motif* may be seen in the construction of the verse and especially the fiction which he was soon able to write. In the meantime, he was delighted with the respectable place he had suddenly achieved in society, the apartment above the bank, the piano he hired, the dinner jacket which he wore to parties, and the new friends he made in the bank and at the boarding house. The work in the bank, he found, was done at a speed almost beyond him. He was "too incurably a dreamer to concentrate on figures," but he did his work well and he soon had an increase in salary of ten dollars a month.

On the 9th of July, 1904, he reported to the Kamloops branch of the Bank of Commerce.[4] This town, with a population of fewer than two thousand people, was situated at the junction of the north and south branches of the Thompson River, in the south-central part of British Columbia. It was in the heart of the cattle country. Service probably recalled that Morley Roberts had given a chapter of his *Western Avernus* to "Round Kamloops." Roberts had seen it as "a long straight street of wooden houses, some of them quite handsome structures," upon an elevation above the river.

Service found the move very agreeable. He was a horseman at last, for he acquired a pony and played polo. He "bought a banjo, tuned it like a guitar, and strummed happily." He scarcely ever read a book; literature ceased as far as he was concerned; his versifying muse had deserted him. Some exciting stories of the Klondike came to his attention, and one of the little juniors in the bank had actually won "a sizeable stake" when he had been sent to the Yukon. Service paid little heed. He had allowed the Gold Rush, at its height in 1898, to pass him by, although he had then been near the jumping-off places for the North, whether he was near the port of Vancouver or wandering within reach of San Francisco.

One morning in 1904 he was told by the manager of the bank that he was being transferred to Whitehorse in the Yukon; the date for the move was the 8th of November, 1904.[5] The "outfit allowance" permitted him to dress himself for a new part; he bought a coonskin coat. Then he set out by boat for Skagway—toward the Yukon, where fate held for him fame and fortune beyond his wildest dreams.

# 3 The Yukon, Song and Story

If millions of people are still able to identify 1898 as the year of the Yukon Gold Rush, Service must be given some of the credit for making it memorable. Yet he cannot be numbered among the adventurers who toiled on "the trail of ninety-eight." Prospecting and exploration had begun in the Yukon before he was born, and in August 1896, just before he had left Vancouver Island to take the vagabond trail to the South, Robert Henderson, George Cormack, and some Indian companions, had discovered gold near Rabbit Creek (Bonanza). The news of the great strike had reached San Francisco and Seattle in the summer of 1897.

Service arrived in Whitehorse late in 1904, in the middle of the decade of 1901-1910, during which the population of the Yukon dropped from 30,000 to 9,000. A tourist bulletin of the Territory, issued recently,[1] reports that "the creeks began to give out and gold was discovered in Alaska. . . . Small mining operations were abandoned and

31

taken over by big companies and the hundreds of
men with their picks and shovels were replaced by
monster sized dredges churning up the gravel beds
of the creeks." Service saw such mines working
night and day.

For the details of his career in Whitehorse, one
must turn to his first autobiography, *Ploughman of
the Moon.*[2] Although winter began soon after he arrived, he found himself entering upon one of the
happiest periods of his life. During the six months
of cold weather he joined, moderately and somewhat shyly, in the entertainments, skating, tobo-
ganning, and dancing of the established society of
Whitehorse. This was different from the life of the
town's "Settlement"; "he didn't think," he said, that
in his three years there, he "ever tasted a drop of
hooch."

He enjoyed both companionship and solitude.
He and the teller, Harold Tylor, a brilliant and
popular boy, lived with the manager of the bank
and his *chic* and dainty wife. At last Service had a
home in Canada, and the conversation was full of
good humour. The manager, who had been an adventurous sea captain, was a good talker, "a virtu-
oso in slang." No doubt he taught Service the use of
the Yukon vernacular. Service was always a listener
and observer. He saw, rather than participated in,
the rough life of the Settlement, for after all, he
had the dignity of belonging to an institution
where money, the goal of all Yukon enterprise, was
handled.

In the short summer season of little more than
five months, Whitehorse was a bustling "gateway to
the North." "From the Outside," Service wrote,
"came the inflowing tide of workers resuming their
jobs and residents returning to their homes." The
steamboats moved again after the deep freeze of
the winter, and "every train brought new crowds

going into the Interior." For Service, the bank
clerk, it was a busy time in the office. Yet he had
opportunities for recreation: tennis even at midnight, for there was little darkness; swimming and
walking in the woods, for here in the North he
found beauty both winter and summer.

Personally, he was dedicated to building up a
nest-egg in his own savings account. The greatest
satisfactions he knew in the North came in long,
lonely walks in the summer and "loafing and
dreaming"—now quite creative reverie—in the
winter. "It was an incubation of all worth while in
[his] life." He realized "the poetry of his surroundings" even before he found the words.

So Service passed his first two winters and two
summers (1904-1906), and then the momentous
year of the Sourdough poems was at hand. With
the end of the summer of 1906, the teller was
transferred to Dawson, and Service replaced him,
happily realizing that his friend was "nearer his
marriage" and he himself, with a thousand dollars
in his account, nearer "his freedom." The composition of "The Shooting of Dan McGrew" described
in a subsequent chapter of *Ploughman of the Moon*
may, therefore, be given a date in the autumn of
1906. Legends about the origin of the poem have
grown up in spite of Service's own matter-of-fact
explanation, which, of course, characteristically included the ministrations of luck or fate.

He had been dallying with amateur theatricals,
entertaining other people with recitations of
"Casey at the Bat," "Gunga Din," and "The Face on
the Bar-Room Floor," and sending a few verses to
the *White Horse Star*. The editor of this paper asked
him to do a piece for a church concert. "Give us,"
he said, "something about our own bit of earth."

Service planned to write a dramatic ballad, but
he had no theme except "the old triangle, the faith-

less wife, the betrayed husband." He sought blankly for "a new twist" until he decided to introduce music—the piano! On this Saturday night there was revelry in the bars. Into his mind popped the key line, "A bunch of the boys were whooping it up." Although it was late at night, he decided to retire to his teller's cage to work on the poem. His movements woke the ledger-keeper who had been sleeping in the guard room. The young man shot at what he thought was the shadow of a burglar. "Fortunately," Service wrote later, "he was a poor shot or the *Shooting of Dan McGrew* might never have been written." With the shot still ringing in his ears, he completed most of the rhymes and the lines of the poem before five o'clock in the morning.

The most significant and probably the most neglected aspect of this ballad "of crude reality and the culture of the common lot" is the basic subject of music.[3] Service had allowed the rhymes given to "the lady that's known as Lou" to compete for attention with the references to the piano playing of the nameless stranger. Perhaps not fully aware (at the time) of the sophisticated use of "musical suggestion," he employed it effectively. Later he wrote a terse statement of shrewd self-criticism: "it suggests the power of music to stir the subconscious and awaken dormant passions."

The first passion aroused by the stranger's music was hunger for companionship in the night and under the stars in the icy world of the "Great Alone":

> the gnawing hunger of lonely men for a
> home and all that it means.
> ................................................................
> A woman dearer than all the world, and
> true as heaven is true.

"Then on a sudden the music changed, so soft that you scarce could hear," and became the "crowning cry of a heart's despair."

Finally, "the music almost died away . . . then it burst like a pent-up flood/And it seemed to say, 'Repay, repay' ".

Before the music stopped with a crash, it woke "the lust to kill, to kill."

Fear of sudden death prevailed as "a woman screamed" and bullets spat within the room; and all the aroused emotions mingled in echoes as Lou kissed the dead stranger, and "pinched his poke."

Bowing to the prudish notions of the White-horse establishment, Service did not recite "Dan McGrew" at the church concert.

A month later he wrote his second ballad, "the result of an accident." At a party which he happened to attend uninvited, he was playing his favourite role of observer, when he watched a fat man, "a big mining man from Dawson . . . smoking a big cigar with a gilt band." The miner told a story of a prospector "who cremated his pal." There was a humorous twist in the surprise ending. Service records that he did not join in the laughter, for he had a feeling that "here was a decisive moment of destiny." Excited, but not beyond words, he walked in the brilliant moonlight and started to compose the rhymes on this "perfect ballad subject," beginning with the lines[4]

> *There are strange things done in the midnight sun*
> *By the men who moil for gold;*
> *The Arctic trails have their secret tales*
> *That would make your blood run cold;*
> *The Northern Lights have seen queer sights,*
> *But the queerest they ever did see*
> *Was that night on the marge of Lake Lebarge*
> *I cremated Sam McGee.*

Before he went to bed, Service composed the whole ballad, all the way through to Sam's remark from "the heart of the furnace roar, . . . it's the first time I've been warm." In the morning he put it down on paper.

"McGee," he said later, "was to be the keystone of [his] success." Yet at this time he put his ballads away in a drawer. As luck would have it, he did not commit them to immediate printing, and thus to eventual obscurity, in the columns of the local newspaper. He continued the walks which suited the rhythms of his own esthetic and verbal excitement. The awe-inspiring beauty of his natural surroundings now flooded into his rhymes, which were usually "two-syllabled." On the heights of Miles Canyon, "I have gazed on naked grandeur where there's nothing else to gaze on" popped into his head and developed into the now famous "The Call of the Wild."

The drama of adventurous men was becoming merged in ballad form with paeans to natural beauty. Man brought life to the North, and the North lent some of its dignity and importance to the struggles of man, even of little men. This was to become the hallmark of Service's unique achievement as a poet. "The Spell of the Yukon" and "The Law of the Yukon" followed in the same impulse of "exultant joy" and "the intense gusts of living." Here, at last, was the heart of Service expressed in the full power of his own words. So he developed rhetorical, but memorable, recreations of life in the Canadian Yukon—vast, cold, hard, savage, magnificent, alluring, beautiful—a frontier of adventure for exiles from cities. The Northern wastes were no more blank: they were given a meaning, an individuality, a language, and symbols of man's restless endeavour.

The arrangement of the selections in this first book of Service's poems appropriately gave prominence to these hymns about the "law," the "spell," the "call," and the "lure" of the wild. "McGrew" and "McGee" occupied a position in the middle of the volume. One finds only a few such dramatic monologues in Service's first collection. Even in "The Parson's Son" and "The Rhyme of the Remittance Man," balladry serves the purposes of song rather than of narrative. This Whitehorse book was, indeed, appropriately entitled *Songs of a Sourdough*—chiefly lyrics *by* an experienced resident of the prospecting community rather than ballads *about* the miners.

As an anti-climax, after the opening selections of high inspiration, there was a considerable scattering of pieces, evidently bookish in origin, which look like earlier poetic experiments that Service dared now to expose to the public. His reading had made him familiar with treatments of sin and sorrow in Poe, Verlaine, and "decadent" poets of the English 1890s. Certainly there were "fallen" women to be sentimentalized about in Whitehorse, but the image with which Service expressed the governance of fate in "The Harpy" came from Edgar Allan Poe:

> *Fate has written a tragedy; its name is*
> > *"The Human Heart."*
> *The theatre is the House of Life, Woman the*
> > *mummer's part.*
> *The Devil enters the prompter's box and the*
> > *play is ready to start.*

In "My Madonna," the woman from the street is "shameless, but, oh so fair!" and the portrait for which she was a model now hangs in a church. This ironic little poem, like "Quatrains" and some of the other songs in the *Sourdough* book, betrays its origin in the sentimental literature of the late Victorian period. Vice is treated with tolerant irony, but within a point of view of moral responsibility, of Presbyterian origin probably, which Service had never surrendered. In "The Woman and the Angel" the Devil is blamed for these opinions heard by every generation:

> *We have outlived the old standards; we have*
> *burst, like an over-tight thong,*
> *The ancient, outworn, puritanic traditions of*
> *Right and Wrong.*

So the *Sourdough* book became something of a catch-all for Service's tentative first efforts at authorship. At least two of the selections had seen print. "The Song of the Wage-Slave"—a work of real strength—had been written when Service was drifting among derelicts on the outskirts of Los Angeles in 1898. "The Old Log Cabin" had been sent from Cowichan, British Columbia, to the editor of the *Whitehorse Star* and printed in that paper on May 10th, 1902;[5] Cowichan is west of Duncan on Vancouver Island, and may be a clue to the location of the big ranch and store where Service worked at that time, apparently not without an early interest in the Yukon. Finally, there were other poems which reflected the Old School Tie community of Duncan, and the imperial wars in Africa—with the almost inescapable influence of Kipling. Among these are "The Younger Son," "The March of the Dead," "Fighting Mac," and "The Tramps,"—probably inevitable results of reciting for his friends such popular favourites as "Gunga Din," "Casey at the Bat," and "The Face on the Bar-Room Floor".

The desire to be a narrator as well as a singer

was growing, however, even before public response to "McGrew" and "McGee" brought him the confidence to follow the dictates of his own talent. Rhapsody about nature was not enough. He reports in *Ploughman of the Moon* that in Whitehorse he had definitely turned to writing "of human nature, of the life of the mining camp, of the rough miners and the dance-hall girls." "Vice," he said, "seemed to me a more vital subject for poetry than virtue, more colourful, more dramatic, so I specialized in the Red Light atmosphere." It was a promise of additional dramatic monologues, but *Songs of a Sourdough* is not the place to find them. They belong in the sequel, *Ballads of a Cheechako,* published two years later as a result of Service's observations at Dawson City, in the very heart of the old prospecting extravaganza.

When he had collected all the manuscripts from his bureau drawer, Service decided to squander his hundred-dollar Christmas bonus "in egregious authorship." He "visioned a tiny volume of verse which he would present to pals"—a hundred copies printed at his own expense. A fellow Scot refused to buy a share in the venture for fifty dollars: it would have brought him fifty thousand! Service retyped the pieces and sent them to his father in Toronto (his parents, Robert and Emily Service, and their family had emigrated to Canada, where the elder Robert died shortly thereafter). The poet's father delivered the manuscript to William Briggs, the Methodist Church publisher in Toronto (later the Ryerson Press).

The poems found their first enthusiasts in the typesetting room, and seventeen hundred copies were sold in Toronto "from the galley proofs alone." The publishers offered a contract, at a ten per cent royalty on a book to sell at one dollar. Service's first cheque amounted to one hundred and seventy dollars. *Songs of a Sourdough* would go into its fifteenth impression during 1907. In the same year it went into its first British edition; in 1910, the third year, there would be the twenty-third impression, by T. Fisher Unwin of London, and in 1917, the thirty-sixth, by the same firm. In the United States, Barse & Hopkins of New York and E. Stern and Company of Philadelphia published the collection under the title of *The Spell of the Yukon and Other Verses* (1907). The first copies arrived in Whitehorse with the Spring mail of 1907. Service hailed it with rapture tempered at first by little commendation from his fellow townsmen; it was the summer tourists who brought news of his fame.

He kept on saving money—his goal being five thousand dollars—and doing his job in the bank. When the third winter came, he was given three months leave with pay, and his residence in Whitehorse came to an end. This winter holiday, the first of two vacations in the South during a total of eight years in the Yukon, was not a success. He evidently took a steamer out of Skagway to land at Vancouver. He had little to say about his residence there in "a boarding house with twenty boarders and one bath"; he was little known there as a celebrity, and he made few friends. In fog and rain he suffered from colds and longed to return to the Yukon.

His wishes were granted, and the bank sent him back, this time to Dawson, as teller. He was to report for duty there on April 4th, 1908.[6] Once more he made the trip by steamer to Skagway, and by train to Whitehorse, happy to greet the "great silence of the snows." It was late March when he travelled six days by open sleigh, in a temperature

*Public Archives of Canada*

A street scene in Dawson, Yukon Territory, July 1899.

of thirty degrees below zero, from the town he knew to Dawson City, where he hoped to "write the essential story of the Yukon from the inside." It was certainly the best place for that ambition: on August 17th, 1896, gold had been scooped out of Bonanza Creek, eleven miles from Dawson, and had started the Gold Rush to that city.

A modern brochure of the Klondike Visitors Association[6] refers to the attractions of those old great days in the 'Paris of the North,' boasting elaborate hotels, theatres, and dance halls rivalling those of San Francisco and offering entertainment by Diamond Tooth Gertie, Klondike Kate, Tex Rickard, Jack London, Rex Beach, and Alex Pantages. Also "beautifully appointed churches, a Governor's mansion, and hospitals, rose side by side with log cabins and canvas-roofed stores." Without pausing for breath, the writer of the brochure describes "palatial river steamers laden with luxury goods, vintage wines, first editions for private libraries, French gowns, show girls, church workers, doctors, chefs, dog mushers, spilled their cargoes onto the docks of Front Street." Everything was rough, loud, and gaudy. And, of course, there were the miners. This was what Athol Meldrum is alleged to have seen and what is described in Service's novel *The Trail of Ninety-Eight:* he felt "an intense vitality charging the air"; the general effect of the architecture held for him none of the elegance suggested by the brochure: "all," he said, "was grotesque, makeshift, haphazard"—"oddly staccato." There was a great deal of corruption, extravagance, drunkenness, vice, riches, and disappointments. Gold production had reached a maximum in 1900, but had declined by 1907.

When Service arrived in 1908, the population had dropped to four thousand and Dawson was on

*Germaine Service*

Robert Service at work in his Dawson cabin.

the way to becoming a ghost town. "Less than a third of the dwellings were occupied." The last of the dance halls was closed down soon after he arrived; there were, however, many residents left to spin yarns of the old days, and Service found his ghosts of the past as he roamed through the places which had made history ten years earlier.

His cheques for the *Sourdough* now came from both Canada and the United States in amounts jumping from fifty to one hundred and fifty dollars. He made four thousand a year from his first book. He now became a deliberate writer and planned a sequel; *Ballads of a Cheechako* was "self-conscious, premeditated." Not a collection of scattered verse, it was built on a definite plan, written on a schedule, "from midnight until three in the morning" because his companions "whooped it up" until late at night. It was completed in four months of 1908. His material, he said, had "been in the bag." There was nothing miscellaneous about it; all of it dealt realistically with the Klondike. A glance at it now confirms his own opinion that "there was little lyric verse, and most of the descriptive ballads were over-long." It expressed the spirit of the Yukon, he said, "more than anything I have done."

He was now in a position to bargain with publishers. William Briggs complained about the "coarseness of his language" and his "lack of morality." A rival firm bid for the book, but Service agreed to let Briggs have it on their proviso that he should drop the objectionable ballad of "The Tenderloin" for a sweetener of an extra five per cent on royalties. The book was given the modest title of *Ballads of a Cheechako,* from a Yukon term derived from Chinook jargon for a newcomer, a tenderfoot. It was copyrighted by the author in 1909 and

in that same year was published by Briggs in
Toronto, by Barse and Hopkins in New York, and
E. Stern in Philadelphia. It soon brought him three
thousand dollars.

Service thought that these new ballads were an
"improvement on [his] first work, and as usual [he]
revelled in rhyme." He was still, as he said in the
opening poem, the dreamer and "the thrall of
Beauty" but more determined to listen to "the
pregnant voices of the Things That Are"—

> *The Here, the Now, the vast Forlorn around*
> *us;*
> *The gold-delirium, the ferine strife;*
> *The lusts that lure us on, the hates that hound*
> *us;*
> *Our red rags in the patch work quilt of Life.*
> *The nameless men who nameless rivers travel,*
> *And in strange valleys greet strange deaths*
> *alone;*
> *The grim, intrepid ones who would unravel*
> *The mysteries that shroud the Polar Zone.*

The promise of the ballads in *Songs of a Sourdough* comes to fruition in Service's special way in
the Dawson monologues. In the "yarns" we are told
of Ole Olson (the sailor Swede); the Dago Kid;
claw-fingered Kitty; Windy Ike and the-man-who-
had-no-name; Pious Pete; Blasphemous Pete
(MacKie); One-Eyed Mike; Tellus, the master
smith; Hard Luck Henry (Smith); the man from
Eldorado and Muckluck Meg; a murderer and
thief; the Prospector; the blacksheep of the
Mounted Police; the telegraph operator; the wood-
cutter; Gum-Boot Ben; Clancy of the Mounted Police; the man lost in the blizzard; and the "brotherhood of men that know the North." One of the
poems, a comprehensive survey of the prospecting

*University of Washington Libraries*

One of the many saloons that sprang up in Dawson to cater to thirsty gold-seekers and townspeople.

army which came to Dawson in the days of the
Gold Rush, indicated even more extensive plans
for the future and supplied the title for Service's
first novel, *The Trail of Ninety-Eight.*

During twenty-four months (1908-1910) after
this poetic outburst, Service wrote nothing. He did
his work as a teller, conscientiously if not rapidly,
and enjoyed social events as well as his solitary
walks. His five thousand goal had been reached,
and a new one of ten thousand was in sight. Then
"grandiose dreams" of writing a novel of the gold
rush took on a practical form. This is how he
planned *The Trail of Ninety-Eight:*

> *[It] must be an authentic record . . . tragic and
> moral in its implications, a vivid scene on a
> big canvas. The characters must be types, the
> treatment a blend of realism and romance. . . .
> My book would be the only fictional record of
> the gold rush. I would document myself like a
> Zola. I would work on old sourdoughs and get
> their stories. I would brood over the scenes they
> described till they were more real in my mind
> than in theirs. It would be I who suffered their
> hardships and exulted in their triumphs.
> Vicariously I would be one of the vintage of
> ninety-eight. I would re-create a past that
> would be lost forever.*

The principal character was named Athol Meldrum, conceived as a Scot whose early wander-
years in America were more or less parallel to Service's experiences. Before going to the North,
Meldrum visits San Francisco, works in a construction camp, carries a banner in Los Angeles, picks
oranges, goes to San Diego, and takes passage in
steerage back to San Francisco. Meldrum then
takes part in the Gold Rush of '98, as Service per-

sonally did not, and Meldrum's character unfolds
in ways only in part suggestive of Service's own nature.

"I wrote in the first person," the author explained, "which is the easiest way":[7]

> *To avoid any charge of false psychology I*
> *exploited certain phases of my own character in*
> *the person of my hero. I made him a romantic*
> *dreamer, unable to come to grips with reality*
> *and at odds with his environment. He was*
> *sensitive and unpractical, a fumbler and a*
> *weakling. Yet he had a certain moral strength*
> *and courage. . . . In short, like myself, he was*
> *destined to failure; but while I escaped by a*
> *fluke, I took it out on my poor devil of a hero,*
> *and gave him the works.*

Meldrum is reputed to have sailed for the
North from "Klondike-crazy" San Francisco on the
4th of March, 1898, to join the great army of
would-be Yukon miners numbering about 28,000
by May of that year.[8] All the "human dregs" of that
city's "dead-line" were said to be on this ship bound
for Skagway in Alaska. Whether or not Meldrum's
journey was by way of the "Inland Passage," it
probably was given some of its colour by Service's
own first trip to the North in 1904. For both of
them, Skagway was the point of debarkation. Meldrum saw there "indescribable bustle, confusion,
and excitement," "a frantic eagerness for the gold-
trail," "hundreds of scattered tents", saloons, dance
halls, gambling joints, and "lawlessness."

In this town, Service's Meldrum and his
friends had to choose between two routes to Whitehorse in the Canadian Yukon, the most famous of
which was through Dyea over "the grim old Chilcoot with the blizzard-beaten steeps." Meldrum

*Yukon Archives*

Dance-hall girls in Paradise Alley, Dawson. "Women were everywhere, smoking cigarettes, laughing, chaffing, strolling in and out of the wide-open saloons." *The Trail of Ninety-Eight* went by way of the "less precipitous, but more drawn out" Skagway trail. Service, in 1904, missed the rigours of travel through the mountain barrier, but he was able in his novel to describe Meldrum's alleged experiences in memorable language:[9]

> *The spirit of the Gold Trail. . . . It was based on that primal instinct of self-preservation that underlies our thin veneer of humanity. It was rebellion, anarchy; it was ruthless, aggressive, primitive; . . . Of pity, humanity, love, there was none, only the gold-lust, triumphant and repellent. . . . Yet there was something grandly terrible about it all. It was a barbaric invasion, an army, each man fighting for his own hand under the banner of gold. It was conquest. . . . I realized how vast, how irresistible it was. It was Epic, it was Historical.*

The famous pictorial details of "The Human Chain" struggling over the Chilcoot Pass are also there:

> *men with haggard, hopeless faces, throwing their outfits into the snow and turning back broken-hearted; men staggering blindly on, exhausted to despair, then dropping wearily by the trail side in the bitter cold and sinister gloom; weaklings, every one . . . [some venting] their fury and spite on the poor dumb animals . . . a sacrifice on the altar of human greed.*

In 1904, Service rode in a Pullman on the White Pass and Yukon railway which was completed from Skagway to Whitehorse in 1899. He gave scarcely a page of *Ploughman of the Moon* to an account of his own trip. He "was glad that he had not been one of those grim stalwarts of the Great Stampede."

*Public Archives of Canada*

Gold-seekers ascending the summit of the Chilkoot Pass (1898-1899). "Like a stream of black ants they were, between mountains that reared up swiftly to storm-smitten palisades of ice." *The Trail of Ninety-Eight*

Finding that the work of writing this novel required seclusion, Service refused promotion to a
manager's post at Whitehorse, and left the Dawson
bank on November 15th, 1909.[10] He rented a cabin
on the hillside overlooking Dawson and the valley
of the Yukon. In spite of the bitterly cold weather,
he did not entirely forsake his friends in town, but
he lived alone in his cabin with a cat and a huge Si-
berian bearhound called Mike. He studied the
scenes and listened to more old-timers' yarns; in
the Carnegie library he discovered old files of the
*Dawson News.* All through the winter, he puzzled
over a beginning for the novel until the incentive of
an offer of a fifteen per cent royalty put him to
work for the best part of a year. Any reader of the
novel can now observe that imaginative description
was easier for him than the invention of a plot. "I
let the scenes pass before me," he said, "as if they
were being unreeled on a film and just wrote them
down as I saw them." Deciding that he "would have
to inject romance into it, invent a plot, and create a
villain," he was responding to a taste for melodrama which was also characteristic of early Hollywood films.

In an amusing passage in *Ploughman of the
Moon,* he remembered how he had assembled his
hero, Athol, his heroine, Berna, and "a bunch of
extras" together on his porch to help him create
"conflict, suspense, drama, all that makes a story
punch." Athol, who is "a bit of a bum," suggests
that he be allowed to make his fortune in the gold
fields, marry Berna, and live happily ever after.
"Nothing doing," Service had replied, "The happy
ending is out. I've got to make it tragic. I've got to
consider the art angle. This 'boy meets girl' situation is all wet. I can never let you have a fade-out in
each other's arms nor give you a baby to suggest
domestic bliss."

"But you're not going to kill me," said his heroine, who was assured of being "pure" because his publishers would not accept her if she were tarnished; she had to be "an inspiration to virtue." Such were the difficulties of giving her "the breath of life" for, after all, her name had been borrowed from "the brand on a can of condensed milk." In addition, she had to have uncommon powers of resistance against "a menace" yet to be invented. His characters, Service felt, never wholly responded; not even Athol turned out to be more credible than the "synthetic villain."

His sardonic view of his hero is not evident in the early part of the novel, where Athol's experiences as a vagabond on the West Coast strongly suggest the author's own experiences. The descriptions of the Yukon and its people, rivalling in prose the language of *Sourdough* and *Cheechako* poems, kept Service himself involved in the novel. Wherever romance enters with Berna, the author's tongue-in-cheek narrative takes over and he himself bows out.

Athol's interest in Berna and her feeble father grows, develops into love, and involves him emotionally in the net of intrigue drawn around innocent Berna by the unwholesome Madam Winkelstein and her squinting husband, and by the libertine Jack Locasto, who wants her as his mistress. Berna escapes to Athol, and they plan to marry. But melodrama is not yet played out. Garry, Athol's brother, arrives, and, disapproving of his brother's liaison, contrives to make a show of seducing Berna so that Athol will "realize how worthless she was . . . her love . . . a sham, a pretence to prey" on him. But Berna and Athol have actually been man and wife. Garry and Locasto die in a burning hotel; Berna saves Athol's life and then disappears. Athol returns to Scotland.

This plot, with some changes in the action and with excellent pictorial support from Gold Rush scenes, became a Hollywood movie in 1928 under the direction of Clarence Brown. Ralph Forbes played the part of Larry (Athol in the novel), Dolores Del Rio that of Berna, and Harry Carey that of Locasto. It was presented at the Astor Theatre in New York on the 20th of March, 1928, before an audience which a reviewer described as "critical and appreciative";[11] he also found the film to be "highly exciting, not without its melodramatic moments and its flashes of symbolism." There was "a wonderfully realistic fight" between Locasto and Larry.

Service's plot in *The Trail of Ninety-Eight*, started him on a career as a novelist of the coarse, the violent, the mysterious, the spectacular, and the "absurd", akin to (but not likely to be revived in) the fiction of the 1970s. The experiments in irony were further developed in *The Pretender*. The lyrical prose of the setting has become part of the poetic glamour with which the old Yukon past is invested in song, story, and the literature of tourism.

Who has not been stirred by such names as these which Service added to the roll call of romance: the Klondike, the Skagway trail, the Chilcoot, Paradise Valley, Lake Bennett, Tagish Lake, Lake Labarge, the Yukon River, the Squaw Rapids, Dawson City, Bonanza, Eldorado, the Malamute and other saloons, Gold Hill, the Palace Grand? In this novel, as in the songs and ballads, Service was the phrase maker of the Gold Rush: "the Spirit of the Wild," "the Golden Magnet," "the great Cheechako army," "the gold-lust," "the Great Stampede," "Klondike or Bust," "the Trail," "the Great White Land," "the Men of the High North," "the

Brotherhood of the Arctic wild," "the Argonaut boats," "the ice-worms," "the Klondike Kings," "the Man with the Poke," "the Land of the Strong."

Recognition of Service's merits as a verse writer has been obscured by the title of "Kipling of the North," popularly conferred, and inappropriately but cheerfully borne by him for many years. It is, of course, true that he was somewhat obligated to Kipling's verse, and that he never denied a certain amount of indebtedness. That amount, however, must be measured against the failure of critics to find in Service's works anything but meagre evidence of imitation, and against Service's own explanations in *Ploughman of the Moon*.

In the autobiography, Service placed this matter in the perspective of his whole endeavour as a popular poet.[12] He had learned his craft—not so much in college classes as in private reading and reciting—by absorption of the lines and rhymes that the English-speaking world was reading and reciting during his career. It is one thing to be a simple imitator—which he was not—and another thing to be what he was—a rhymer steeped in the contemporary fashion of balladry. For knowing his business he should not be scorned.

*Ploughman of the Moon* shows how well he knew the tradition of popular verse and contemporary practice of the art. *Barrack-Room Ballads* (1892) was not the only book which he read. He had begun with Burns as a boy in his grandfather's home. Browning and Tennyson were "big stars" for him when he was in his 'teens, a clerk in a Glasgow bank eager for poetry; he carried "a tiny Tennyson" and "a brownie Browning" in his pocket to read ". . . at every odd moment—even on the toilet seat." So he laid foundations in the Victorian tradition, and developed the habit of always carrying books in his pocket, even when, on vagabond journeys, he had little else.

Attracted to form, he had bought "a series of pocketable books . . . published under the title of the Canterbury Poets." One was devoted to "French patterns," another to sonnets, and he was soon composing imitations of Keats and of Austin Dobson's ballades. He had also learned to speak intelligently about certain French authors, particularly Verlaine. Some of his later writing reflects "decadent" literature of his youth. He soon found verse making more congenial than formal poetics. In the lighter tradition, which he then favoured, he admired Thackeray and Thomas Hood. Poe was evidently first among his American authors. All of these charmed his ear for rhythm, and he imitated what he heard. "I never read a poem I admired, but what I tried to emulate it," he wrote late in his life.

Long before he went to the Yukon, he had turned to writers closer to his own time and to his own interests: Stevenson on romantic vagabonding, Kipling on the trail of adventure, and the Americans Bret Harte on California and local colour and Eugene Field on folksy sentiment. Like Meldrum in *The Trail of Ninety-Eight,* he rejoiced in the books he had taken everywhere on his travels: his "beloved Stevenson," his "great-hearted Henley" and his Thoreau. It is easy to see how these writers blended into a background for Service's efforts, and provided an incentive for joining them by writing in accord with his own ideas and modest ambitions.

When Service was interviewed by a *Toronto Star* reporter in September, 1912, he confessed that he had been largely influenced by Kipling. In *Ploughman* he identified Kipling as his "first inspiration."

"I had read a lot of poetry," he is quoted as saying, "but Kipling was a particular favorite, and I must have fallen into a form moulded on his almost unconsciously." The implied distinction between influence on form and influence on substance remains an important one. When Service started writing in the Yukon, Kipling had turned to imperial wars which were of no great concern in the far Canadian North. If the book in Service's pocket, from which he "would rant poetic stanzas to chipmunks and porcupines" was by Kipling, it must have been a copy of *Barrack-Room Ballads.* Anyone who attempts to find more than a few direct borrowings by Service from Kipling must sense how foreign most of the latter's subjects—except the general topic of adventure—can appear to North American readers, and no doubt did appear to Service, a man naturalized in the North as no other poet could be. In "The Nostomaniac," published in *Rhymes of a Rolling Stone,* the author is dreaming by the fire glow, his "Kipling flat on his knee." But *Kim* falls on the floor as he finds himself responding to the call of life in the North.

His second influence, Service said, was "the Ancient Mariner," and later Bret Harte and Eugene Field. When he arrived in Dawson City after his first vacation from the Yukon, he aspired to become "the Bret Harte of the Northland." Eugene Field had pleased him with blunt "Saxon speech." Summing up, Service made this point: "My material was uniquely my own, so that I might be forgiven for modelling myself on others." In other words, he was an eclectic poet, one of many writers on both sides of the Atlantic who pioneered in unconventional non-aristocratic, non-bourgeois rhyming—which was, Service confessed, the work of patient toil.

Some of the confusion about what Service accomplished as a poet of the North can be diminished if one concentrates on a few of the *Sourdough* hymns and ballads, and the *Cheechako* monologues. He is said to have created the Myth of the North, but it is more accurate to speak of a *Myth of Man in the North*. The struggle of man against forces too strong for him is archetypal; *hubris,* precarious lonely adventure, and the ironies of heroic failure or of illusory success are concerns of a tragedy. These were also Service's concerns when he interpreted restless human adventure in a wilderness, whether natural or man-made. The belief that destiny is stronger than self-will also added the perspective of irony, which redeems the too-obvious pathos of low-mimetic, dramatic monologues such as "Sam McGee." The amazing public response to the comic and the tragically romantic in Service's work may indicate a popular awareness of the main lines of literature which his apparently artless balladry has obscured for many critics.

# 4 Farewell to the North

When his novel was "complete in a bulky and untidy manuscript," Service decided to deliver it personally to his publisher.[1] This vacation on the "outside" was to be spent, not on the west coast, but in Toronto and New York. Once more he travelled by steamer to Vancouver, and eastward, in the "unaccustomed luxury" of a Pullman, to Toronto; there on April 30th, 1910, he was interviewed by a reporter for the *Star Weekly*. William Briggs was still his publisher in Canada, but Service also went on to the United States to make arrangements for his novel with Dodd, Mead of New York. Although in the Yukon he was a solitary writer, preferring to work in the privacy of a secluded place, he wished to see the great city in which sophisticated literature was being produced. The cynical use of the observations which he made there may be found in the opening pages of his second novel *The Pretender,* which will be discussed in our next chapter.

His "Civilization Interlude", beginning in the

late spring of 1910, was extended into "a little stroll as far as New Orleans." The Poet of the North followed once more the lure of the vagabond trail leading southward to the sun. He actually began his trip on foot with a pack on his back, and he went as far as Philadelphia. There he bought a Pullman ticket for New Orleans, where he hoped to discover "colour . . . gaiety and poetry." Finding that city covered by grey skies and not quite up to his hopes, he left for Havana. Here he found "effervescence, colour, emotion" in the streets, in the open-air cafés, and "no colour bar, no puritan inhibitions," "sheer animal enjoyment," "picturesqueness, freedom, glamour—the Latin way of living," "in slip-shod loveliness where pleasures [were] many and duties [were] few." When he grew tired with the heat, and bored with the South, he "longed for the snow and tonic air of the North."

Meanwhile (in 1910) William Briggs copyrighted and published *The Trail of Ninety-Eight, a Northland Romance*, with illustrations by Maynard Dixon. The artist's four pictures bore these captions:

*We were in a caldron of fire. The roar of*
*doom was in our ears*

*"No," she said firmly, "you can't see the girl"*

*Then, as I hung half in, half out of the*
*window, he clutched me by the throat*

*"Garry," I said, "this is—this is Berna"*

The New York editions of the book, also copyrighted in 1910, appeared with the same illustrations by Maynard Dixon. The photographs which readers may remember viewing in later reprints of the novel were taken from scenes in the Metro-Goldwyn-Mayer movie directed by Clarence Brown in 1928.[2] The book and the film were then

Germaine Service

Robert Service's mother, about 1911.

displaying a revised spelling of the title: "Ninety-Eight" had become " '98."

It was late autumn in 1910 before Service arrived in Canada to visit his mother and family whom he had not seen for fifteen years and who were now living on a prairie farm in Alberta. Winter had begun: there was deep snow, sunshine, and cold "far below zero." The family had been very happy in their struggle to settle in a Scottish community in the new land. Robert spent the winter of 1910-11 in a "prairie idyll." With the coming of spring, the North called this restless man again, and he took to the road on foot. But he returned to the family home, for he had plans to attempt a return to the Yukon by the long and dangerous "old Edmonton trail."

One needs a map stretching into the Arctic circle to appreciate the length of the journey which Service had chosen to take instead of the usual route by train to Vancouver and by steamer to Skagway. His description of this trip in *Ploughman of the Moon* (pages 343-382) is one of the best and most exciting stories he ever wrote in prose, for it is not only a personal geographical record of an important part of the Canadian northwestern territories, but it is also a modest, yet dramatic, revelation of the daring, courage, and endurance of the poet. Had he not had the fortitude of a northern explorer, and physical strength carefully built up through all his North American years, he would not have survived the terrible dangers of this trip. If he had not gone back to the Yukon by this route, his reputation as the poet of the Gold Rush would have been enough. Choosing as he did, he deserved, but did not acquire, another title of distinction as a poet of the great Mackenzie River. *Rhymes of a Rolling Stone*, his third book of verse, was writ-

ten in Dawson after his arrival there; but it is
not strictly a Yukon book—it is an "Arctic" book by
Service's own admission that he "definitely abandoned the Yukon and [his] new work concerned
the Mackenzie basin and the Arctic." Among his
friends he bragged of the "greatness of the Mackenzie Valley as compared to the Yukon," for the
man who had gone into the Arctic circle "strutted it
over the man from the subarctic".

There can be no substitute for a reading of
Service's own account of his journey as it is found
in *Ploughman of the Moon*. The land he passed
through is still so little known by most readers as to
require consultation of a good map. The general
directions from Edmonton were northwest by
north to a point near the delta of the Mackenzie on
the Arctic Sea, then west and south over the Divide
to the Yukon River and Dawson. The distances
travelled through wilderness, largely on water, ex-
ceeded 2,000 miles.[3]

Spells of easy life on board steamers alternated
with intervals of hardship on rivers and portages.
It all began with a two day trip of a hundred miles
by stagecoach to Athabasca Landing, which was
then "a huddle of shacks." After that, canoes were
required by Service and his companions—an English mining engineer and his brother (a naval officer) in one canoe, and Service, a Swedish doctor,
and an Indian guide in the other. They paddled
down stream (northwards) about nine hours a day
and camped in the open at night; Service had a little mosquito tent and blankets. Before evening on
the second day, they went through an "oil region,"
where they saw a flaming jet of natural gas rising
twenty feet in the air.

The next afternoon they caught up with a
dozen barges of the Hudson's Bay Company, for

they were then, and would be for many days, on established Company routes and passing Company posts. They were given space on one of the barges, and Service was content to watch the Indian rowers and the widening Athabaska river carry them along. For amusement he joined the engineer in the hazardous sport of running rapids in a canoe. Such experiences later provided material for ballads in *Rhymes of a Rolling Stone.*

At Fort McMurray there was a steamer, providing him with a stateroom of his own, on the way to Smith's Landing, where there was a twenty-mile portage to Fort Smith, and another steamer going to Fort Simpson. At that fort, an unfortunate flair for comedy prompted him to ride an ox into the Indian village, only to find himself shunned as a government agent. So far he appears to have been following, chiefly by water, the route of the present-day Number 2 road north of Edmonton.

At Great Slave Lake he bought a very fine birch-bark canoe. Here his account begins to lack specific details, but there is mounting evidence that he stored up narrative material which he later used in the *Rolling Stone* volume. "At last," he records, "we left Fort Simpson and embarked on the mighty Mackenzie . . . a river voyage . . . easy, intimate, varied and safe." What it meant to him and his next book is stated in a very significant passage:

> *We visited a score of forts and met many*
> *Factors who hailed from the Hebrides.*
> *Highlandmen make the best officers of the*
> *Company, because they are hardy, used to*
> *loneliness and good traders. It is a saturnine*
> *life that takes men of determined sanity to*
> *endure it. These Hudson's Bay posts were a*
> *mine for the story-teller, but the grim men who*
> *manned them had no sense of the romance of*
> *destiny.*

> *Fascinating books have been written on*
> *this trip. I made copious notes, intending to*
> *add another volume to the list, but other events*
> *crowded on me and I never got round to it.*
> *Imaginative work ousted mere reportage of the*
> *Wild.*

The material was used, not in prose beyond the *Ploughman*, but certainly in the *Rhymes*.

The goal of this long voyage northward was Fort McPherson, near the Mackenzie Delta at the junction of the great river and its western tributary, the Peel. This was well within the Arctic Circle, and not far from present-day Aklavik and Inuvik. Dawson City was still far to the southwest, over the very formidable barrier of the mountainous Divide. Service now heard repeated warnings, expressed by such authorities as the experienced factor and a Mounted Police officer, against attempting the cross-country trip. Even the Indians refused to take Service and his canoe part-way to the headwaters of the westward-running rivers. The trail was said to be almost impassable. Yet Service was still determined to accept the challenge of this adventure, and allowed the last Company boats of the season to go south without him.

By chance he learned of a scow named the *Ophelia* which was going his way, en route to Dawson. Its skipper was a Captain McTosh, a free trader, accompanied by his comely wife, and also by his quarrelsome, cigarette-obsessed mate, Jake Skilly (who had the experience of trapping white fox on the Mackenzie Delta). Two Indians started out with them.

They paddled westward up the Peel River to the mouth of the Rat, and then along that river in a plague of mosquitoes to where the water was rough and then shallow. "Tracking" became necessary: for Service this meant adopting "a job that would

have made a Volga boatman look like a slacker."
The half-ton *Ophelia* had to be hauled up to the Divide and over to the other side by five men (sometimes assisted by the captain's wife) proceeding
along the bank or in the water, pulling the boat by
tow-ropes harnessed over their shoulders. Service
described his role as that "of a yoke-ox and a
beaver, with the working capacity of both." In all
his life he had never worked so hard. They usually
spent twelve hours a day at this task, most of the
time in the water.

There were all sorts of additional difficulties.
On some days, progress amounted to only half a
mile. The scow had to be unloaded, carried over
portages, and then repacked. The Indians quit and
returned to Fort McPherson, leaving the voyagers
in doubt about their route; missing the way would
have meant disaster. At one particularly dangerous
point on the Rat River, where there was a strong
opposing current running out of a canyon, Service
nearly lost his life. He was jerked off his feet and
carried downstream, backward toward the east. He
was completely covered by water, and his back was
bumped over boulders. He was saved by "one snag
of stone" which held the scow long enough to enable Jake to gain control. Service's fabulous luck
prevailed again, and he tackled the mountain barrier again with "a high heart."

The great mountains closed around them and
only more good luck prompted them to select the
branch line which would take them toward the little
lake at the height of the Divide. A portage over the
last intervening mile required vigorous pushing of
the scow over the tundra, which presented problems whether dry or wet. Finally, Service carried
his precious canoe, the *Coquette,* over his head, "in
the Indian way," to the cold clear water of the little

lake, where he and his companions camped at the top of the Divide. Joyfully he now took to the canoe and tried to go down alone on a swift-running stream, in great danger of boulders in the whirling waters. When he reached the next river, he rejoined his companions of the *Ophelia* only to find more trouble: Jack and McTosh were quarreling and Jake was going mad because his store of paper for cigarettes was nearly depleted.

Service decided to risk the rest of the trip alone in his canoe; the beginning, down the Bell River, was an "idyllic" experience—largely a matter of drifting two hundred miles through gentle and warm country to the junction with the Porcupine River. It was a "river of dreams." "Most of my dreams were of Dawson, my cabin and the work I planned to do. On the Mackenzie I had gathered a lot of material that was different. As I paddled I mulled over this and saw ballads in the making. How I longed to get at them!"

But Jake turned up again, becoming dangerous now because of a desperate shortage of cigarettes, when Service was within three days of Rampart, the trading post on the Porcupine. The crisis came with Jake's very last piece of paper as they saw Rampart just ahead of them. Access to the Post was denied them because of a smallpox epidemic raging there. Tension grew, and crazy Jake, fondling his axe, presented a real threat to Service's life. As luck would have it—unexpectedly as always for Service—a small stern-wheel steamer was stuck in the river not far beyond the post, and Jake got paper for his tobacco. Service arranged passage for both of them up the Yukon. "Lucky for me you struck that snag," he said, "for I've had enough of paddling for the rest of my life."

The boat was a pleasant place to resume a leisurely existence. He borrowed a guitar from the steward and composed a song that the deckhands learned and sang for years afterwards. It was called "When the Ice-Worms Nest Again." Composition may have amounted to offering new words for an earlier Northern song, for the fictional Pote (Dawson spelling for Poet), whose lyrics "seemed to be original, even improvisations" had used this stanza in *The Trail of Ninety-Eight* (already in print in 1910):[4]

> *In the land of pale blue snow*
> *Where it's ninety-nine below,*
> *And the polar bears are dancing on the plain,*
> *In the shadow of the pole,*
> *Oh, my Heart, my Life, my Soul,*
> *I will meet thee when the ice-worms nest again.*

Another version attributed to Service has this refrain:

> *Oh! Oh! Oh! In the land of ice and snow*
> *With an igloo for a palace*
> *'Neath the Rory-boryalis*
> *She'll be waiting for me I know,*
> *Oh! Oh! Oh! And it's there I want to go,*
> *For my dream it is to stroll*
> *In the shadow of the Pole*
> *With my little Eskimo.*

Clearly, he had not lost the common touch, and he was full of plans for ballads when he arrived in Dawson, happy to be in the ramshackle little "near-ghost" town again, and back to his "pathetic, deserted" cabin with "the moose horns over the porch" stretching out arms to welcome him. He resumed his bachelor life and his solitary tramps in the woods and on the hills. It was a wholesome life, with plenty of leisure and exercise to make his "muscles ripple," but even here there could be danger in his restless desire for adventure.

One of the last chapters in *Ploughman* tells how

he started out for Gold Run, a distance of nearly
fifty miles. Going back the next day, he took a different trail and became almost fatally lost and fa-
tigued by travel in the snow. He was saved at a terrible price when he came upon a solitary cabin, occupied by a strange man who slowly revealed himself—at the business end of a shotgun—as
"Cannibal Joe" who, it was rumoured, had eaten
his partner a few years before. With the weapon in
his hand, the crazy man told his own story. Like the
Ancient Mariner, he made Service listen to the true
version: Bob had died of starvation, and the sequel
was, *"I fed him to the dogs and I et the bloody dogs."* Fiction and experience became blended in Service's
*Rhymes of a Rolling Stone.* Fate was the dominant
theme.

Yet the Mackenzie Valley ballads were written
with great deliberation. Service's habits of work are
nowhere outlined more clearly than in this para-
graph:

> *I used to write on the coarse rolls of paper used
> by paper-hangers, pinning them on the wall
> and printing my verses in big, charcoal letters.
> Then I would pace back and forth before them,
> studying them, repeating then, trying to make
> them perfect. I wanted them to appeal to the
> eye as well as to the ear. I tried to avoid any
> literary quality. Verse, not poetry, is what I
> was after—something the man in the street
> would take notice of and the sweet old lady
> would paste in her album; something the
> schoolboy would spout and the fellow in the
> pub would quote. Yet I never wrote to please
> anyone but myself; it just happened I belonged
> to the simple folks whom I liked to please.*

Service worked at his ballads during the winter
of 1911-12 and added to his gallery of Northern
characters the names of Eddie Malone (who had a

grammyphone at Fond-du-lac); Athabaska Dick from Lac Labiche; Tom Thorne; Barb-Wire Bill; Happy Jack ("the lunger"); Flap-jack Billy (who was given the "Cow Juice Cure" for alcoholism); Chewed-ear Jenkins, the bald man (and his wife, Guinneyver McGee); the Squaw Man, and little Laughing Eyes. There are other nameless ones, and more men dreaming nostalgically of loved ones than in the earlier books of rhymes. The occasional exercises in conventional lyrics are equally sentimental.

Some of the poems reflect particular events recently experienced. One may account in this way for the vividness with which Service described "the hell of frenzied foam" in "Athabaska Dick"; the deep contentment given by camping in the wilderness in "The Song of the Camp-Fire" and "While the Bannock Bakes"; the threat of murder in "The Dreamer"; and the sad farewell of "Good-Bye, Little Cabin". The whimsy of the Northern raconteur appears in the rescue of the whiskey in "Athabaska Dick", the surprise ending of "The Cow-Juice Cure", and the shifting fortunes of "The Chewed-Ear Jenkins Hirsute Propagation Syndicate." The concerns of a literary man appear in "Prelude" ("I sing no idle songs of dalliance days"), "The Ghosts" ("For oh, the supremest of our art are the stories we do not dare to tell"), and "The Scribe's Prayer" ("When from my fumbling hand the tired pen falls").

"The Mountain and The Lake" is worthy of the poet who wrote the *Sourdough* hymns to the North and the wild:[5]

> *I know a mountain thrilling to the stars*
> *Peerless and pure, and pinnacled with snow;*
> . . . . . . . . . . . . . . . . . . . . . . . .
> *My peerless mountain, splendid in her*
>   *scorn. . .*
> *Alas! poor little lake! Alas! poor me.*

*Provincial Archives of Alberta*

Service's cabin in Dawson (1908-1912). "Its moose horns over the porch were like arms stretched out to me." *Ploughman of the Moon*

Patronizing references to the native people of
the North were all too prevalent at that time, and
Service can be blamed for tolerating the "squaw-
man's" words for living with a native girl as a "dark
disgrace." The ballad fortunately ends with a warm
tribute to "little Laughing Eyes." One also wishes
for permission to change a line in "Little Mocca-
sins" ("Your mother was a half-breed Cree, but you
were white all through"), because this little song is
almost completely charming:[6]

> Come out, O Little Moccasins, and frolic on
>     the snow!
> Come out, O tiny beaded feet, and twinkle in
>     the light!
> I'll play the old Red River reel, you used to
>     love it so:
> Awake, O Little Moccasins, and dance for me
>     to-night!

Service finished his new *Rhymes* in the spring
of 1912, but he lingered in his beloved cabin until
the last boat of the summer was leaving for the
South. A vacation would then begin, and he would
go to the romantic South Seas of his favourite, Robert Louis Stevenson. But the editor of the *Toronto
Star* had other plans for this adventurer. There was
war in the Balkans, and Service was asked to go to
far-off Europe as a war correspondent. Acceptance
brought him deep regret on leaving the North—
temporarily, he thought. In truth, he would never
return.

He polished his rhymes during a month or two
which he spent south of Vancouver, while living in
a tent in the foothills of the Olympic Mountains. In
September he was in Toronto: the *Star* reported his
presence there on the 20th of the month.[4] Probably
he made his second visit to New York at this time:

*Rhymes of a Rolling Stone* was published in that city in the same year (1912).

New York was almost certainly his port of embarkation for Europe,[7] since he crossed the Atlantic in a German luxury liner. His "inferiority complex" and the haughtiness of the ship's officers and passengers disturbed and offended him; here he was treated as "just a lousy little nobody." When he reached Naples—whether directly by sea, or by train—he revelled in the "riot of colour" and the "roar of life" of a Latin city, as he had, for a time, in Havana. He went to Brindisi by train, and across the Aegean in moonlight. "So by seas of cornflower blue," he wrote, "I came to ten-tiered Istanbul with its domes and minarets gleaming in the sunrise."

Here, in a fine café, while dressed with his accustomed flair ("a fez cocked over one eye, a gilt-tipped cigarette between [his] lips and a gorgeous concoction called a *Susanna* at [his] elbow") he met Doctor Dilly. The doctor had become his boss, for Service had decided that he could get closer to the war front as a Red Cross man than as a correspondent without any kind of uniform.

His explorations in old Istanbul persuaded him that it was "sinister," and he had little stomach for the danger of taking a load of rice to a cholera camp. Very soon, a monocled Colonel who disliked "newspaper pests" fired him from the service. When the police became inquisitive about his papers, he ended his Turkish war experience by taking sudden leave on a Rumanian steamer going across the Black Sea.

At every stage in his journey toward Paris, he found material for anecdotes and for future use in his fiction. On the way to Bucharest, in the smoking room of the Orient Express, he met Sir Pelham

Pelham, who was apparently determined to take over the "raw colonial" (Service) and make a sophisticate of him, especially with regard to available women. Pelham constantly cast himself in the role of a cinema Casanova. Through him, Service learned about the sexual games played by these men and women of leisure in Europe. He also learned how to observe and makes notes about them without close involvement: he purchased, and placed on the mantelpiece of his room in Bucharest, a portrait of a beautiful woman to which he could point with pride as "My wife." Becoming acquainted with Pelham's English mannerisms, he was conscious of his American slang and tried to improve his own manner of speaking; he went so far as to see himself wearing a monocle. Pelham's example kept him busy at warding off seduction by predatory women.

Seeking a quiet view of "common" people, Service took a third-class seat on the train to Budapest. Crowded in by an unsophisticated family group, he was sickened by such close contact. After spending the Christmas season of 1912 in Budapest, he went on to Vienna, where Sir Pelham turned up again, still in quest of amorous adventures. One of these turned into a cinematic intrigue involving the nobleman and the wife of a Spanish Count. Service now saw Pelham as a kind of play-actor in an artificial world—indeed as a character for "international" fiction—useful to keep in mind when stories for the "slicks" would be written. "I was inclined to think . . . ," Service wrote, "that most of his [Pelham's] conquests existed in his imagination. I was not to meet him again for a number of years, but even then he was to appear in the character of a cardboard Casanova."

Pelham appears to have affected Service's subsequent fiction by the identification of his lifestyle with the half-real, half-artificial tone of popular storytelling—the literary world into which the man from the Arctic was trying to enter with his personal integrity intact. He felt so soon after his arrival in Europe that he was expanding his knowledge of the technical devices of ambiguity. Athol Meldrum of *The Trail of Ninety-Eight* had revealed too much about his author; more finesse, more artfulness, was demanded now. *The Pretender* (1914) shows the results.

"Cardboard characterization" solved many of Service's technical problems, and "pretence" would shape his plots, as he gave the public the melodrama and the love scenes which were in popular demand. "Cardboard" became one of his ways of masking himself as he wrote two-dimensional stories in which a third dimension of subjective involvement on the part of the author was veiled. He practised the art of letting his characters in song and story tell their own tales—in the first person point of view—but he generally planted clues which pointed away from himself.

# 5 The Literary World

In the spring of 1913, Service completed his leisurely trip from the Balkans and arrived in Paris.
He entered this radiant city of his dreams with rapture. For fifteen years Paris would be his "only
love." Names and scenes about which he had read
leapt at him: Hugo, Daudet, Zola, Notre Dame, the
Tuileries, the Place de la Concorde, the Champs
Elysées, the Arc de Triomphe, and especially
Montmartre and Montparnasse. There, he
thought, he would enjoy all the "inducements to
live in a foreign land—freedom, strangeness, irre-
sponsibility, romance and adventure."[1]

Choosing the Latin Quarter, where he could
observe the bohemian life of artists and literary
folk, he took "a four-franc mansard"—a room
under the roof in an old hotel on the Quai Voltaire.
He looked down the Seine towards its lacework of
bridges and over to the Louvre on the opposite
bank. He could see the spires of Sainte Chapelle,
the towers of Notre Dame, and the boats and

77

barges on the river. Here he dreamed alone, but he also set out to make "human contacts," not like a tourist eager for autographs but like a sensitive and patient journalist making notes of all he saw and heard.

His early bohemian period might be characterized (in English terms) as still Edwardian or Early Georgian, pre-dating the changes of the war. Like his own character James Madden of *The Pretender,* he began by wandering freely in the Paris of the past, looking for ghosts of old bohemia, not only by way of books but in "a mania for old houses."[2]

*I do not mean houses of historic interest, but ramshackle ruins tucked away in seductive slums. To gaze at an old house is to me more fascinating than trying to realise romance you know occurred there. I examine doors studded with iron, peer into curious courtyards. . . . I step in the footprints of Voltaire and Verlaine, of Rousseau and Racine, of Mirabeau and Molière.*

It was the decade before the expatriate era of the Americans Hemingway and Fitzgerald in Paris, which would also be the scene described in Canadian books by Morley Callaghan and John Glassco. Service frequented places which the lost generation would make familiar in their books: the Closerie des Lilas, the Dôme, and the other famous places where writers sat and talked.

The excitement of his discovery of Paris is recorded in two brief chapters in *Harper of Heaven,* entitled "The Latin Quarter" and "Bohemian Days." A more complete account of his first year in France is still buried in the files of the *Toronto Star* between the dates of December 6th, 1913, and January 10th, 1914. The general title of the series was "Zig-Zags of a Vagabond." There were six weekly instalments, each one illustrated with photographs, and bearing respectively the subtitles of "Paris, A City of Alienating Seduction," "The Lure of the Latin Quarter," "Montmartre, The Monstrosity," "Afoot in Fontainbleau," "Baedekering in Brittany," and "The Fisher-Folk of Finistère."

He was evidently only half a bohemian, as he had been half a hobo. At this time, during his first Parisian year, while he was describing the beauties of the Seine, the streets and the life of the city, he still felt the superior beauties of the open road and the French countryside. He left Paris on a "push-bike" with no definite goal.[3] On the first day he "did fifty miles with enthusiasm, the second, ten with a sore fanny. From then on [he] averaged twenty, depending on the distance between pubs." So, with pauses to write articles, he went through Normandy to Brittany:

> *The Breton country charmed me, and I lingered lazily in that Land of Wooden Shoes. I wrote of the fisher-folk of Finistère, and its cider-swigging sons of the soil. I did some swigging myself, in oak-panelled taverns or sunny seashore* buvettes, *and the more I saw of Brittany the more of it grew on me. From the sky-blue sardine nets of Douarnanez to the grim cairns of Carnac; from the quaint* coiffes *of Concarneau to the brilliant brocades of Landerneau; from the fantastic off-shore rocks to the grey stone cottages with their oak-fringed farms. How I loved it! . . . Then one day I happened on a village that seemed lovelier than all. In a sea coast famed for its charm its beauty took my breath away. . . . But somehow my eyes always went to a little red-roofed house that stood on a sea-jutting rock . . . . it seemed to call to me saying: "I am empty and sad. I want to be lived in. Please take pity on me. Buy me."*

Impulsively, yet shrewdly wearing the garb of a poor man—"stained pants, a ragged shirt, a broken straw hat and disreputable sandals"—he secured an option on the house and furnishings for the knocked-down price of ten thousand francs, and produced that sum to the owner's consternation and surprise.

Service's characteristic mingling of motives is well illustrated in this anecdote: "freedom with some security, wealth with an appearance of poverty, adaptability with deep-seated longings, romance with hard realism, depth of sentiment with theatrical poses." He returned to his garret, sharing his memories of Lancieux with his programme for literary success in Paris. He later wrote:[4]

> *Oh, won't I have the leaping veins, and*
> *tawny cheek and sparkling eye*
> *When I come back to Montparnasse and*
> *dream of Finistère.*

He was back in Bohemia, but not quite of it. There was something foreign in his Scottish/North American outlook, however much he affected bohemian roles. Professionally, too, he was an observer and actor. "I was never happy," he said, "unless I was playing a part. Most people play one character in their lives; I have enacted a dozen and always with my whole heart."

His first good friends were a married couple, almost his own age, who had come from the Canadian West to paint and make etchings in Europe. His description of this unnamed pair seems to fit the careers of Frank Armington (born in Fordwich, Ontario in 1876) and his wife Caroline Helena Wilkinson (born in Brampton, Ontario in 1875).[5] They had met and married while both were studying art in Toronto, and then, from 1901 to 1905, they had taught and painted in Winnipeg. They

*Germaine Service*

The *Coquette*, a birch-bark canoe which Service purchased at Great Slave Lake, July 2, 1911. "A gaudy patchwork of purple, scarlet, primrose and silver, it danced on the ripple as lightly as a leaf." *Ploughman of the Moon*

*Germaine Service*

Early days in France. Mr. Frank Armington, Mrs. Caroline Armington, and Robert Service at Lancieux, 1913.

lived in Paris and painted in Europe until the late 1930s. "For years," Service wrote, he "enjoyed their gentle friendship." (Caroline died in New York in 1939 and Frank in 1941.) Through them he met other painters.

So Service began to cast himself as an artist. He took lessons in the studio of Colorossa in the Rue de la Grande Chamière, modestly attended a "life class," and dressed the part in a "broad-brimmed hat with a butterfly tie and velveteen jacket." During this first year in Paris, he learned to "loaf on the terrace of the Dôme Café, waggle a smudgy thumb as [he] talked of modelling, make surreptitious sketches of [his] fellow wine-bibbers and pile up [his] own stack of saucers." The Louvre "lulled [him] to somnolence," and "on the other hand, excessive modernism irritated [him]." He observed "the long-haired freaks who spent their time between the Dôme and the Rotonde."

When he shuttled "from an atmosphere of Art to one of Culture," Service was not disconcerted by the approval or disapproval of his verse by critics or by friendly journalists. James Stephens, poet of *Crock of Gold,* was a friend who "loftily" described the Yukon ballads as "very good newspaper verse." Edmund Gosse, the eminent biographer, admired the binding of *Rhymes of a Rolling Stone,* but did not open the book. Other writers whom Service met were Gellett Burgess, an American humourist; James Hopper, writer of short stories; Neil Munro, "the only Scots author with more than a local reputation"; and romantic-looking Glasco Ibanez, the novelist exiled from Spain. The journalists whom Service mentioned were "Adam of *The Times,* Jerrold and Grey of *The Telegraph,* MacAlpine of the *Daily Mail,* Hill of the *Montreal Star,* Donahue the Australian, [and Peter McQuattie of the *Morning Post*]."

*Germaine Service*

Robert Service and Archibald Kerr Bruce, "Peter McQuattie," (on the right) with Breton fishermen, Lancieux, 1913.

Peter McQuattie was the name which Service gave in *Harper of Heaven* to his best friend, who has now been identified by Mrs. Service as Archibald Ker Bruce.[6] Robert and "Peter" had met on the terrace of the Dôme when Ker had introduced himself as "a journalist of sorts and I would like to write an article on you for the *Morning Post.*" Service saw him in terms of "a Skye terrier, for he had a shaggy moustache and friendly blue eyes under a thatch of eyebrow." He spoke with a decided Scots accent although he had been in France over twenty years after he had given up schoolteaching in Scotland. He was a convivial talker who rarely wrote anything except his articles for the Sunday paper. Early in the war, he took on a new sense of responsibility as manager of Reuters news agency in Paris, and he married "a Scotch lassie, a girl sweetheart," whose mother, a widow, was very wealthy. Eventually, but still in the 1920s, "Peter" and his wife had a villa in Vence, on the Riviera, "a Rolls and a chauffeur, and about a dozen other domestics."[7]

Service enjoyed particularly the quiet moments of his life, and he began once more to write. His articles were not given to name-dropping and gossip about the elite of the book world. Although he was at first preoccupied with describing Paris as if no sensitive writer had seen it before him, he paid sympathetic attention to men and women who had become failures, and he expressed his disgust with the time-wasters and "sodden sybarites" of the Latin Quarter.

Bohemians were good stock-in-trade for a story writer. Even in Dawson he had found a few of these to serve as a target for observation, fictional contrivance, and sardonic mockery. Chapter VI of Book III of *The Trail of Ninety-Eight* (1910)[8] reveals his first public attempt to exercise a kind of satire which he would later refine and exploit in his first European novel, *The Pretender* (1914). The Dawson episode opens with Athol Meldrum talking to Ollie Gaboodler in a little log cabin overlooking the mining town. Gaboodler bears the local title of Pote (the misspelling is deliberate); he is a professional "ghost-writer" of novels and poems, and he advertises,

> *In Memoriam Odes a specialty.*
> *Ballads, Rondeaux and Sonnets at modest*
> *    prices.*
> *Try our lines of Love Lyrics.*
> *Leave orders at the Comet Saloon.*

Gaboodler admits that he is a "farceur" with a hope of becoming "the Spokesman of the Frozen Silence, the Avatar of the Great White Land." He has written a book *Rhymes of a Rustler*, over which critics had ranged from admiration to abuse:

> *They said I'd imitated people I'd never read,*
> *people I'd never heard of, people I never*
> *dreamt existed. I was accused of imitating over*
> *twenty different writers. Then the pedants got*
> *after me, said I didn't conform to academic*
> *formulas, advised me to steep myself in*
> *tradition. They talked about form, about classic*
> *style and so on. . . . I can write in all the*
> *artificial verse forms, but they're mouldy with*
> *age, back numbers. Forget them. Quit studying*
> *that old Greek dope: study life, modern life,*
> *palpitating with colour, crying for expression.*
> *Life! Life! The sunshine was in my heart, and*
> *I just naturally tried to be its singer.*

Several other men join in the conversation of this "Bohemian Circle," but nothing they say is worthy of the maturing Service except the Gaboodler passage, in which he adopts the age-old and still modern theme of the poet as a misunderstood and comic figure—whether named Pan, Lycidas, or Gaboodler-Service. An almost classic example occurred years later, in 1942, when Service was in Hollywood. He was cast as "the Poet" in a tiny part in *The Spoilers*, a film made from a story of the gold rush by Rex Beach. "Once I played my very self in a cinema drama," he wrote, "and the Studio people were dissatisfied. They told me: You are not the type."[9]

It is not stretching the point too far to find in Meldrum's bohemian companions an anticipation of James Madden's acquaintances described in *The Pretender* (published by Dodd, Mead in 1914, Service's second full year in Europe). This novel is concerned with literary circles in New York, London, and Paris. The sequence of events, the love affairs, and the other adventures of the central character, James Madden, are, of course, fictitious, and the light thrown upon Service himself reveals chiefly his impressions as an observer. They are given life by personification, dramatization, exaggeration, satire, sardonic mockery, absurdity, and sentiment.

The arrangement of all this material for the purpose taxed his powers of organization much more than his first novel, *The Trail of Ninety-Eight*, had done. Exposure to new scenes, people, and events, especially in France during 1912 and 1913, involved him in new problems of composition. Since he was living the book as well as writing it in 1913, he wished to play the game of fictional, yet subliminally personal, representation. *The Pretender* had to be a much more complicated union of anecdotes than *The Trail of Ninety-Eight* or the books of ballads had been. Madden had to be a much more complex character than Athol Meldrum of the earlier novel, yet consistent enough to hold *The Pre-tender* together and to carry through an interpretation of the literary demands of popular fiction.

It would be a mistake for us to take the second novel lightly as a piece of workmanship, or to neglect, in our biography, the evidence it provides of Service's experiments in technique. The plot is admittedly simple: James Madden dodges matrimony with possessive rich women and with girls more sinned against than sinning until his rhetorical dialogue traps him in a fortunate marriage with Anastasia. Then he learns how to become a good husband and a writer of stories in the bohemian Latin Quarter of Paris. Service's practice in the use of anecdotes, however, permits him to introduce the subtleties of carefully planned irony. The "pretender" has many meanings which coalesce in Madden.

The title could have been in the plural because none of the persons in the novel, indeed not even the author, is what he pretends to be; perhaps it is in the plan to suggest that none even knows what he is. Ambiguity in detail and effect becomes a shaping force in this fiction. A "pretender" is also one who aspires, one who seeks a self-respecting way to both artistic and popular success as a writer in established cultural environments. The vicissitudes of adjustment to people and ideas offer endless opportunities for ironic or satiric treatment—farcical in absurd mistakes, comic in the pride of the dilettantes, humane in dramatizations of unclassified complexities of individuals. The business of fiction is thus carried on, not without conscious artifice.

A special meaning of "pretender" is that of a dreamer who refuses to separate reality from fantasy—who sees reality fantastically and fantasy realistically. Service uses contrivances of ambiguity in incident, characterization, and "point of view" which confuses the central figure's identity with the author's, until the reader does not know what is Madden and what is Service. Exaggeration and melodrama, which are narrative techniques appropriate to literary invention, belong, one must suppose, to the fictitious person of Madden. Yet the author cannot shift all responsibility for excess and absurdity to the mind of Madden, for it is undeniably certain that all these things, and Madden himself, are Service's brain children, his choices, his fantasies, and all these were passed through *his* mind as they became expressed in words.

The author's use of masks in *The Pretender* is unusually complicated. He professes to have a "first-person" narrator in Madden, although he reserves the right to neglect the straw man when the most serious commentary is to be made. Madden's adventures usually reflect nothing more intimate than Service's assumed and sardonic view of his own external relationships. The narrator has two faces because Service, who is neither wholly roughneck nor sophisticate, is displaying a second face to his readers. James H. Madden is "a man of affairs," but he is also "J. Horace Madden," "dilettante and dreamer," reflecting, but not duplicating, Service's own experiences. One example of a purely fictional contrivance appears in the story of Anastasia's degraded parentage and early career; it may be of some use in a sub-plot, but it conveys no truth at all about the respectable and charming French girl whom Service married in 1913.

Complexity is further compounded by the realization that Madden also wears another mask as "a maker of books"; his pseudonym is Norman Dane. Dane appears to reflect more of Service as literary aspirant than Madden does, and is more readily available to the author of *The Pretender* for direct statements about life and literature. "Like a serene over-soul I watched them, I, philosopher, life critic." Whose speech is this? Madden's, Dane's, or Service's own? As if these were not enough dimensions of authorship, we shall see that Madden/Dane wrote some of the chapters of *The Pretender!*

For the purpose of governing the structure of the novel, Service uses consecutively three different settings. One's final impression, however, may be that there is primarily only one, and that is Paris; New York and London are then merely introductory. Service gave forty pages of *The Pretender,* bearing the subtitle of "A Story of the Latin Quarter," to New York, fifty-two pages to London, and all the rest of the book to Paris. His observations of New York may have been gathered at an earlier date, when he took his manuscript of *The Trail of Ninety-Eight* to his publishers. The satiric *tour de force* which opens *The Pretender* was probably built upon the "civilization interlude" (between periods in the Yukon) later described more directly as "New York Pattern" in *Ploughman of the Moon.* His observations of London literary life had evidently been limited to frequenting the bookshops, dreaming in the sanctity of the British Museum's Reading Room, and sentimentalizing the lot of the poor as he walked the streets.

In the "New York Pattern" he confessed that he must have looked boorish or bearish—"Yukonized"—when he arrived in that city. He "talked the vernacular of the mining camp and gloried in its slang." He "had never been sophisticated" and now he was "on the brash side," contemptuous of civilization, cities, and the smooth ways of society. "Sa-

loons were more in [his] line than salons." He
trusted people too simply, and lost his purse to a
thieving Pullman porter. Although he had money
in the bank and a good address, "the National Arts
Club," to go to in Manhattan, he looked uncom-
monly excited, raw, solitary, and credulous. To his
publishers he appeared commonplace, "not at all
what [they] expected." He did not even know the
meaning of *nostalgia*. His efforts to talk and eat like
a highbrow were unsuccessful. The "literary
crowd" snubbed him and were superior and patronizing. One author said he hoped [Service] was
not going to write "one of those dreadful best-sell-
ers."

There were exceptions. He liked certain
members of the National Arts Club: "Editors
McClure and Bob Davis; novelists Hamlin Garland
and George Barr McCutcheon; poets Madison
Cawein and Will Carleton." In general, however,
he agreed with the manager of Brentanos that
among his fellow writers were many "climbers,
chisellers, publicity hounds." These looked on Service as a "vulgar upstart, writing for the rabble,"
and indecently making a fortune thereby, or as
Quince the critic put it in *The Pretender:*

> *Norman Dane is only a dry-goods clerk*
> *spoiled. No, the point is he is the public, the*
> *apotheosis of the vulgar intelligence. Don't*
> *think for a moment he is writing down to the*
> *level of the mob. He charms the great*
> *half-educated because he himself belongs to*
> *them. He can't help it. . . . I tell you Norman*
> *Dane's an upstart, a faker; to the very heart of*
> *him a shallow, ignorant pretender.*

So Service opened up the problems involved in the
failures and successes of a popular writer, typified

by the careers of Horace Madden and Norman Dane.

The introduction to *The Pretender* had also provided Service with a means of satirizing literary pretenders who had annoyed him in New York. Quince the critic and Vaine the poet are type characters in a comedy of "humours." Quince is "a stall-fed man with a purple face, cotton-coloured hair and supercilious eyebrows;" his humour is the incubation of epigrams and rhetoric, completely drowning "a poor little idea in a vat of verbiage." Fortunately, Quince despises Norman Dane's [Madden's] books enough to name them: *The Yellow Streak, The Dipsomaniac,* and *Rattlesnake Ranch.* May one identify these titles consecutively as burlesques of *Songs of a Sourdough, Ballads of a Cheechako,* and *Rhymes of a Rolling Stone? The Haunted Taxicab,* however, does not seem to mock *The Trail of Ninety-Eight.* Quince's opinions are for sale: he will reverse his decision about Norman Dane's books if Madden will lend him money.

The New York poets whom the Yukoner disliked are depicted in the humour of Herrick Vaine, "a puffy, pimply person, with a mincing manner and an emasculated voice." His verses in *Songs Saturnalian* and *Poems Plutonian* are imitative, yielding "a certain dark-brown taste on the mental palate," and unsaleable. Quince, of course, extracts a free copy from Vaine by asserting that he finds "an indefinable *something* in the Herrick work, a *je ne sais quoi* . . . you know."

The conversations of Quince and Herrick are printed as dramatic dialogue—evidence perhaps of an intention, soon abandoned by Service, to make *The Pretender* a fiction in the manner of a comedy of humours. Another one of the character types is Porkinson, a New York broker, "a philistine, an un-

abashed disciple of the money god" and still another, by contrast, Travers, the proud but honest
painter who, although starving, clings to his ideals
and will not prostitute his art nor sell his latest
painting because he wants to leave it to the nation.
Then there is Dane himself, displaying a rather uncommon humour: he worries about his success,
his income of twenty-five thousand a year. Perhaps
he has indeed made a cheap success by following
the fashion of the day in overworked coincidences,
grafted-on love scenes ("clinch pictures"), and
other easy effects! He has been "imagining romance." It's time "to live a little . . . London . . . garret . . . poverty . . . struggle . . . triumph."

Every woman in New York is also in her humour as she tries to take temporary or permanent
possession of the bachelor Madden, now saying
farewell to his romantic entanglements. Silvia is a
fallen woman of Broadway. Mrs. Fitzbarrington
(he addresses her as Stella, Cora, Nora, Flora, or
Dora) is an aging woman of Harlem who ties a
string on him in the hope of losing her husband.
Miss Boadicea Tevandale of Riverside Drive, a suf-
fragette and heiress of a corporation lawyer, tries
to inspire affectionate memories, because she may
also become a widow. For the time being, she has
offered her heart and her large frame to the el-
derly Mr. Jarraway Tope of "Tope's Never-Tear
Ever-Wear Suspenders." Guinevere, one of the
three sporting sisters, the Chumley Graces, spot-
ting Madden in the steerage of an Italian ship en
route to Europe, makes him her guide and fiancé
when they arrive in Naples.

Service rarely carried Madden's love affairs far
beyond their convenience as transitions, providing
reasons for his hero's hasty departure to fresh
scenes and new experiences. At this point in the

novel, London and Paris beckoned, and it was necessary to rescue Madden from the banality of Guinevere, her sisters, their "poppa," and their intolera-
ble high society. Service's "moving picture
imagination", developed in these very early days of
the cinema, was a useful source of theatrical devices. Innocent Madden is released by Guinevere's
irate parent after the young man is discovered in
suspicious circumstances involving Lucrezia, a
chambermaid. He escapes from these two affairs at
once by going to London, aware that only an obli-
gation to marry Mrs. Fitzbarrington of New York
in the unlikely event of her husband's death stands
in the way of complete freedom.

But Madden's life becomes no less complicated, and events have more serious consequences,
when he deliberately chooses to observe humanity
among the poor of London. He sees the "Great
Grey City" as a place of "Crime and Gloom," where
he sentimentalizes over the rich who have never
really lived, and the poor who have to endure the
terrible Microbe called Fear. This image is person-
ified in "the girl who looked interesting" whom he
watched on the street and in a restaurant in South-
ampton Row, and eventually located as an em-
ployee of a villainous "Professor" O'Flather, proprietor of a (rather symbolic) exhibition of
"Educated Fleas." The girl, O'Flather says, is the
one "wot feeds the fleas." By chance, Madden is
near the Thames and prevents the girl from
drowning herself because she has reached the ultimate fear of being killed by O'Flather for poison-
ing his trained troupe of little actors with "Skeeter's
Insect Powder."

Service does not exploit the potential for symbolism in this melodramatic event, but he does lift
the girl's encounter with Madden to rich signifi-

cance in this novel devoted to the interplay of fact and fiction.[10] In a parable, Service's lifelong exploration on the borderline of reality and invention is exhibited in its perplexing paradoxes.

The girl is French and her name is Anastasia. Her problems are real, and she has no acquaintance with the patterns of fiction which sentimentalize the poor and which might have given an artificial shape to her own sad story. She tells Madden about her fatherless youth, her work in a Parisian embroidery shop, her appendectomy and loss of work in London, her hair "tumbling out," her crying in the night, her weakness, her degrading work for O'Flather, her fear, her despair, her temptation to sell her body, and her belief that death is better than dishonour.

Madden, steeped in imaginative ways of handling events, is disturbed to find her Fact paralleling his Fiction. "How curious," he thinks, "I was under the impression such sentiments were confined to books." She speaks "like a penny novelette." She has been saying the same thing as did Madden's heroine Monica Klein in *A Shirtmaker's Romance*. "But I thought," he warns, "we had decided you were to be Fact, not Fiction."

His advice to Anastasia, therefore, is based on fiction. Survival with dishonour as a woman of the streets is better than death with virtue. Desperate Anastasia accepts this solution as a fact of experience. When she offers to sell herself to Madden, he senses that fact is still matching the routines of fiction, and that the bookish code prescribes a virtuous refusal. Having thus "convicted" himself of virtue, he knows the next step which the actor of romantic roles must take: he must make the grand gesture and ask her to marry him. Girls in books might have reciprocated in generosity and refused. Anastasia accepts for practical reasons.

Madden also had a practical reason which had run parallel to his fictional conduct. The *Gotham Gazette*'s report of the death of Mrs. Fitzbarrington's husband in an accident in New York had raised Madden's fear of the lady's claim upon him as a replacement. Marriage with Anastasia provided permanent banishment of this threat. The credit, which belonged to fact, he shifted to the fiction of the fates. "In what ludicrous ways," he thought, "had they worked out their design." "On what trivial things does destiny seem to hinge! Ah! who shall say what is trivial?" But fact, stranger than fiction, had another shock for him. A copy of the *Gotham Gazette* now reported that Captain Fitzbarrington had survived the accident. Madden's romantic gesture in marrying Anastasia was unnecessary. Together they hurried to Paris where she would be freed from fear and he, as he said, would have "a good chance to learn French."[6]

The move to France did not mean an end either to fact or to romance. Anastasia brought her charm to French domesticity in the Latin Quarter and both of them responded to the inexhaustible glamour of a city which was the goal of artists everywhere. In this environment, Madden found around him an abundance of inspiration for writing as well as a rich supply of material to be observed and turned into fiction. He acquired a splendid meerschaum (encased in a flannel jacket), symbolic of domestic satisfaction, and he grew rhetorical about marriage. "Love," he philosophized, "is an intoxicant. [Marriage] is a part of life's discipline, a bachelor's punishment for his sins. . . . " He decided to be outwardly realistic, practising household thrift, and living within his income from writing.

He was situated now where there was little reason to seek and strain for romantic adventures. For example, his friend Helstern, the Swedish sculptor, tells him the story of the great tragedy in his life; on the eve of the wedding his bride-to-be, trying on her gown, caught it in the flame of a large fire. "In a moment she was all ablaze. Screaming and panic-stricken she ran, only to fall unconscious. After three days of agony she died." The story caused Madden to shudder—not at the story, "but because the incident had occurred in [Madden's] novel *The Cup and the Lip*," written before he met Helstern.

"Alas!" he admits, "How Life plagiarizes Fiction."[11]

Madden now observed rather than participated in, the dramatic events which occurred in the lives of his bohemian acquaintances and which barely required literary heightening. Among these were the melodramas surrounding the artist Lorrimer, the beautiful model Rougette, the villainous Lucrezia, and the absurd Seraphine Guignol of Les Halles. In other lives he saw sentimental roles acted out in reality by the seamstress Frosine, her little daughter Solange, the good-hearted sculptor Helstern, and, in the Madden household, Dorothy, a baby who was born dead. Everything was grist for the writer's mill as he attempted to find success in the contemporary vogue for *realistic fiction*.

Madden is obviously a romanticized and fictitious representation of a type—a caricature—an expatriate writer struggling to sell his literary works about his new environment. He is superficially like Service's sardonic view of his own experiences as an aspiring European author, but without private or intimate details about himself. A question still remains: to what extent is Madden's record of composition and publication in *The Pretender* a reflection of Service's own literary efforts during his pre-war years in Paris?

And what shall be made of Peter McQuattie's early but unfulfilled dream of writing a book about Paris and the Latin Quarter to be called *Youth and a City*? After a period of six months, Service had handed Peter such a book with the words, "Here's your book . . . only I wrote it."[12]

Ambiguity reaches its final triumph if one has doubts that the fictional character (Madden) could have produced books and stories accepted by publishers. Claims are made for a novel called *Tom, Dick and Harry;* a whole chapter of *The Pretender* is given to it. The title was identical with that of the serial written by Mugson, a friend of Service's during his bohemian youth in Glasgow. The setting of the story in *The Pretender* was a desolate moor in Wales, where three men went mountain climbing: Tom, a cockney clerk with dreams of being a writer, Dick, an adventurer, and Harry, an entertainer. They awoke from sleep into mist, only to find that they had slipped back a thousand years and had been made prisoners by strange men. Taken to the king of the country, Tom becomes the royal storyteller and prophet; Harry, the royal minstrel; and Dick, the adventurer who wishes to discover America. They do things in modern ways. Before their vacation runs out, Tom, who has offended the Church, is about to be executed; Dick has married an Irish princess and become an Irish king; Harry has been stabbed by a jealous court jester. It is a dream.

Madden submitted *Tom, Dick and Harry* for publication under the pen-name of "Silenus Starset." It was refused on one occasion with a note from an editor pointing out that "at that time when the taste of the public was all for realistic fiction works of fancy stood little chance of success without a well-known name on the cover." It was accepted, however, by "MacWaddy and Wedge" for their Frivolous Fiction Library, and a great surge of publicity made the name of "Silenus Starset" famous. Incidentally, who were MacWaddy and Wedge?

Meanwhile Madden had written twenty more stories. *The Great Quietus* was another ambitious novel of fantasy; it dealt with the degeneracy of the human race (the "quietus"); a new race began with the birth of a child. The American magazine *Uplift* accepted this story after it had bought the serial rights for *Tom, Dick and Harry*.[13] Madden also began some articles with the general title of *Demi-Gods in the Dust*, "devoted to the last sad days of De Musset, Verlaine and Wilde," and additionally "a series of genre stories of the Paris slums, called *Chronicles of the Café Pas Chemise.*"

Any reader who searched *The Pretender* would have found the novels of fantasy: *Tom, Dick and Harry* summarized on pages 183-189, *The Great Quietus* on pages 278-283. So that much exists as Madden's work. *Demi-Gods in the Dust* is not outlined beyond a few comments: "those strong souls whose liaisons with the powers of evil plunged them to the utter depths." The *Chronicles of the Café Pas Chemise* appear to be covered sufficiently in two chapters of *Harper of Heaven* entitled "The Lower Depths" and "Caught in the Criminal Net." There they are patently Service's own.

But where can one find the twelve articles and stories which Madden or his "secretary" (his indefatigable wife Anastasia) is said to have submitted to English, and perhaps American, journals? There is a list of these titles on page 161 of *The Pretender:*

> *The Psychology of Sea-Sickness*
> *An Amateur Lazzarone*

*A Detail of Two Cities*
*The Microbe*
*How to be a Successful Wife*
*Nurse Gwendolin*
*The City of Light*
*The City of Laughter*
*The City of Love*
*Three Fairy Stories*

These were posted to twelve different destinations in England. In the course of time some of them were accepted. The editor of the *Babbler* took "The Microbe" for one of his weekly Tabloid Tales. "How to be a Successful Wife" appeared in *Baby's Own*, "a weekly Magazine specially devoted to the Nursery." "Nurse Gwendolyn" was rechristened "My Terrible Christmas," and was taken by a cheap weekly. "A Detail of Two Cities," referred to as "the New York-London article," was taken by the Sunday section of the *New York Monitor*. Out of twelve manuscripts, four were sold. Five of the remainder were descriptive articles. "People won't read straight descriptive stuff," Madden decided; "even in novels one has to sneak it in."

It is frustrating to find that the magazines in which Madden is alleged to have published seem to be inventions. A search through lists of English and American journals around the year 1913 has shown only the ingenuity with which Service faked nearly credible names for them. One wonders whether the articles, stories, and novels attributed to Madden in 1913 were ever written, and whether there is in them any information whatever about Service's literary efforts in 1913. Are these titles fictional masks for writing still buried in files of old magazines, or perhaps puzzling clues to experiments forever lost?

The surprising fact is that they can be found in

the source from which they came. If the list is arranged according to the sequence of events in Service's novel *The Pretender*, one finds chapter after chapter which appear to be the very article by Madden we are seeking. The test is worth making, for there is little doubt that we may equate "The Psychology of Sea-Sickness" with Book I, chapter V of *The Pretender*, namely "A Seasick Sentimentalist," in which Madden describes his condition as he crosses the Atlantic.

As one goes on equating, "A Tale of Two Cities" suggests Madden's experiences with authors, critics, and dangerous women in New York, and with Anastasia, "the girl who looked interesting," and who was rescued from the Thames and from solitary despair in London. "The Microbe" is more difficult to place unless it deals with Professor O'Flather and his fleas. The connection of "An Amateur Lazzarone" is established through Lucrezia, a Neapolitan chambermaid who stole Madden's purse but who, in the melee which followed, was claimed as his whore—a device to rescue him from his "involuntary" engagement to Guinevere Chumley Grace (Chapter VI).

In Book II of *The Pretender*, one can find a series of equivalents with nearly all the chapters about the first year of Madden's domestic life with Anastasia in Paris. The series begins with "How to be a Successful Wife," an alternative title for "The Newly-Weds" (Chapter I). Chapter II and the next three chapters, with the very titles on the collective list, describe the attractions of Paris: first the Seine and the Latin Quarter, and after that, (III) "The City of Light" (brilliant lighting on the principal streets and shops on New Year's Eve); (IV) "The City of Laughter" ("watching Paris laugh" at a dance hall and a bohemian corner café); and (V)

"The City of Love" (at the Luxembourg Gardens Madden, Anastasia, and Helstern showing their love for little Solange, daughter of the seamstress). One of the "Three Fairy Stories" may be found in this chapter—the charming tale of the little boy and the Pumpkin King. In the next chapter (VI), there is a horror story told to Anastasia about deranged "Nurse Gwendolin" (who tried to cut Madden's throat with a scissors and succeeded thereby in removing a malignant growth). At this point, one reaches the "list" and the middle of *The Pretender*.

It appears, therefore, that not too much of Madden's alleged production in 1913 has been lost. Perhaps *Youth and a City*, which Service claims he wrote for Peter McQuattie, is actually the whole *Pretender* as we have it. As his Latin Quarter novel was building up, he exploited its ambiguities. Madden said that "Fact plagiarizes Fiction," and Service demonstrated that Fiction plagiarizes Fact.

# 6
# Parisian Idyll, the Great War, and Hollywood

Among the many influences affecting Service's thoughts and activities after he settled down in Paris, possession of "Dream Haven," the red-roofed cottage in Lancieux, was one of the strongest. He now had a home, but he was still a bachelor, and he confessed to Peter McQuattie that he wanted a wife.[1] "I am ready", he said, "for the greatest of all life's adventures—Marriage." He wanted "a wee Scotch lassie who would respect the bawbees." If he couldn't have a Scotch mate, "a French one might do." But nice girls in his circle were rare, and he did not know any. "So I put myself," he said, "in the hands of Fate, hoping for the best."

Fate obliged him one day when there was a parade of soldiers on the Grand Boulevard. Two young ladies were caught in a jostling crowd, and Service performed a rescue for them. They were sisters, daughters of Constant Bourgoin, who owned a distillery at Brie-Comte-Robert near Paris.[2] The younger one was named Germaine; she

103

had been educated at a convent, and she could speak English. Invitations to tea and Sunday trips to Versailles, St. Cloud, and Fontainbleau played a part in the very proper and delicate game of courting this younger girl, whom Service began to vision in the frame of "Dream Haven." His proposal of marriage, however, was definitely unsentimental. If his account in *Harper of Heaven* (1948) may be credited, he said,

> *Say, why don't we take a chance? . . . Let's get hitched. I'm only a poet and as you know poets don't make money, but I guess we can manage to rub along. If you're not scared at the prospect of marrying a poor man let's live in a garret with a loaf of bread and a jug of wine, and we'll sing under the tiles . . .*

Mademoiselle, who had a sense of humour, accepted him. They were married on the 12th of June, 1913, and both began happily to play their "new parts."

Their first residence was the "Rabbit Hutch": "two rooms barely big enough to swing the proverbial cat." Madame possessed what her husband called the "art in handling the male brute," and especially his "egotistic antics" while writing a book. She proved to be a devoted wife and an excellent thrifty housekeeper within the restrictions imposed by Robert's decision to share lessons in bohemian poverty.

The temptation for a biographer to guess at the domestic life of Robert and his wife during these early years of marriage is virtually irresistible. But Service set up proper safeguards when he skimmed over the subject in *Harper of Heaven*, "A Record of Radiant Living." "Had I been writing the story of another man I might have revelled in details of domestic life," he explained, "but as I am

*Germaine Service*

Robert's bride, Germaine Bourgoin, 1913.

*Germaine Service*

Robert and Germaine Service, Paris, October 1913.

telling the history of my own I feel a certain restraint."

*The Pretender* is obviously "the story of another man" (Madden) and "another" woman (Anastasia)—both "cardboard" characters.[3] The novel was written for a reading public that would regard it as a melodrama of the Latin Quarter, exploiting observations of typical and common experiences among the inhabitants of bohemia; the first person method of narrative was literary artifice. Not until *Harper of Heaven* was published thirty-four years later would readers suspect autobiographical involvement in the novel, and then the author's own account confirmed the generality of the fiction at the same time as he hinted at the true and unique characteristics of his own "blessed state."[4]

*The Pretender,* however, remains a prime source for a summary view of the life and scenes of the Latin Quarter as Service saw them, and wrote about them in 1913 or 1914. Discounting Madden's eccentric life and manners, one must regard these descriptions as Service's own work, although they carry the pseudonym of Madden/Dane.

Book II of *The Pretender* opens with rhapsodic pictures of the Seine in late December:[5]

> *Looking down the shining river the arches of*
> *many bridges interlock like lacework, and like*
> *needles the little steamers dart gleaming*
> *through. The graceful river and the gleaming*
> *quays laugh in the sunshine. . . .*

The Hôtel du Monde et Du Mozambique is "a tall, decrepit building that at some time had been sandwiched between two others of more stalwart bearing who now support it." One approached a third storey room by climbing "a winding stairway lit by lamps of oil."

There is relief from its drabness in the nearby opera, "a cinema house near the Place St. Michel, where we go on rainy evenings, usually in our oldest clothes, and joking merrily about opera cloaks and evening dress."

The atrocious "complex" furnishings of the best bedroom of the Hôtel finally drive Madden and his wife out to look for a *logement* in the rue Mazarin, renting for five hundred francs a year. The street is "mouldering," and the apartment is in[6]

> *a gloomy-looking building entered by a massive, iron-studded door. Through a tunnel-like porch-way we see a tiny court in the center of which is a raised space about six feet square. Within it stand a few pots of dead geraniums and a weather-stained plaster-cast of Bellona, thus achieving an atmosphere of both nature and art.*

The apartment requires cleaning and furnishing by a thrifty housewife.

While Anastasia plies her daily routine, her husband, the writer, takes a walk, pausing at times "to fill (with reverence) the meerschaum pipe, which is colouring as coyly as a sun-kissed peach." He coins fine phrases about what comes into view, the Seine, the quays, the "icicle-fringed" *bâteaux-mouche*, the Pont des Arts, the domed Institute, the Ile de la Cité, the Pont-Neuf bridge, the statue of Henri Quatre, "the time-defying towers" of Notre Dame, the statue of Voltaire, the rue Bonaparte, the Ecole des Beaux-Arts, a pawnshop in the rue de Rennes, "the naked cherubs in the centre of the basin in the Luxembourg," preparations for Christmas in the shops of the Boul' Mich' and stalls on the pavement "tenanted by portly, red-faced women."

Madden's wife wears "furs of electric rabbit," and he has "a long, black brigandish cape that has previously been worn by some budding Baudelaire or some embryo Verlaine." In the evening they go down to the "City of Light," the Place de la Concorde, "the jewelled sweep of the Champs Elysées", the Grand Boulevards, the Place de l'Opéra ("a great eddy, flashing and myriad gemmed"), the *magasins* ("blazing furnaces erupting light at every point"). As they walk, they come upon "song writers hawking their ditties," "poor artists peddling their paintings, a 'canvas for a crust'," and "a silhouette man" who turns out to be an old friend, Lorrimer.

Madden is busy with a series of articles on Paris, where he has found "a steady glow of inspiration." "A pure delight in form and colour thrills me," says Madden.

*"I begin to see beauty in the commonest things,*
*to find a joy in the simplest moments of*
*living."*

There is even a charm in shops for vegetables and fish.

At a dance hall at the head of the Boul' Mich', Madden and Anastasia enjoy the colours, shapes, and variety of the people cavorting in the ballroom. There they are introduced to Lorrimer's pretty model, Rougette, who speaks "the *argot* of the Quarter, grafted on to the *patois* of the Breton peasant." From the din of the dance, they retire to a large corner café, where they are surrounded by "all the freaks of the Quarter." There they see Paul Fort, "Prince of the Poets," "the heritor of the mantle of Verlaine;" a peaked-faced futurist poet; a cubist sculptor ("a Russian Jew"); and "an Imagist," "a meagre little man in evening dress," "releasing some of his inspirations." Here they meet

Helstern (who becomes a great friend) and they hear two Englishmen talking about International Peace.

One morning Madden makes the acquaintance of Madame Frosine, a shy, brave, poverty-stricken "human sewing machine" and Solange, her beautiful child. Madden and Anastasia arrange to take Solange to the Luxembourg Gardens to enjoy the sunshine. This is a prelude to incidents of joy and sorrow concerning children born in the Quarter. On another occasion the couple take Solange to "her first sight of the real country" in Barbizon.

When Madden is looking for a different place to live, Helstern shows him a spacious garret in the rue Gracieuse in the Quartier Mouffetard, "one of the least gracious streets of Paris," and, near the rue Saint-Médard, the most disgusting of all, the "headquarters of the *chiffoniers,* the hereditary scavengers." When they find it possible to move from these surroundings, Madden and his wife settle in a better apartment in the Passage d'Enfer. Madden continues his excursions into various parts of Paris. Lorrimer takes him to hear the *chansonniers* of the Noctambules, and Madden himself escorts a wedding party to visit the Catacombs of the Place Denfert Rochereau and then to see a matinée at the Grand Guignol:[7]

> *we would go out on, to me, the pleasantest of*
> *all the boulevards, Montparnasse. We would*
> *walk down as far as the Invalides, and,*
> *returning, sit in front of the Dôme or the*
> *Rotando Café and sip* Dubonnets *while we*
> *watched the passing throng. We mixed with the*
> *groups of artists and students that thronged the*
> *rue de la Grand Chaumière with its gleaming*
> *signs of Croquis schools, where for half a franc*

*one may sketch for three hours some nude*
*damsel with a wrist watch and very dirty feet.*
*Or we spent a tranquil evening in a Cinema,*
*halfway down the Boulevard Raspail, whose*
*cherry-coloured lights saves the people on the*
*apartments across the way a considerable sum*
*yearly in gas bills.*

Since even Parisians required holidays in the country, Madden and his wife spend three weeks on the coast of Brittany at a house called "Dreamhaven":[8]

> *it stands between the poppies and the pines. A*
> *house of Breton granite, built to suffice a score*
> *of generations, it glimmers like some silvery*
> *grand-dame, and its roof is velvety with*
> *orange-coloured moss . . . the old garden*
> *where a fig tree climbs the silvery wall . . . :*[9]
>     *We bade [our jolly Bretons] good-bye this*
> *morning; great, great grandfather Dagorn*
> *herding his cows on the velvety dune; Yyves*
> *swinging his scythe as he whisked down the*
> *heavy crimson clover; Marie stooped over her*
> *churn; Mother Dogarn whose withered cheeks*
> *are apple-bright; the rosy-faced children, the*
> *leaping dogs. We looked our last on that*
> *golden beach, that jewelled sea; we roamed our*
> *last amid the hedges of honeysuckle, the*
> *cherry-trees snowed with blossom, the stream*
> *where the embattled lilies brandished blades*
> *and flaunted starry banners. Last of all, and*
> *with something very like sadness, we bade*
> *good-bye to that old house I called*
> *Dreamhaven, which stands between the poppies*
> *and the pines.*

These veiled allusions in *The Pretender* could not have held much significance for Madame Service at this time, for her husband had not said a word to her about ownership of "Dream Haven". She would soon find out.[10] When the novel was published, Service had not been able to disguise the fact that it would bring ten thousand dollars. It was apparent that he and his "Missus" could afford a holiday, at least as far as London, to deliver the manuscript to Fisher Unwin, the publisher. During this fortnight of a "belated honeymoon" they saw some of the tourist sights and something of London's slumland. Robert visited James Bone of the *Manchester Guardian,* whom he had not seen since school days, and he met Christopher Morley.

After their return to Paris—in order to display his dignity as a poor man in spite of enormous increases in income—Service proposed another holiday for Germaine and himself, a bicycle trip—one bicycle for each of them—through Touraine and the Château Country, to Brittany, in fact to the fishing village of Lancieux, on a cove not far west of St.-Malo.

Here Robert walked boldly up to the little red-roofed cottage with a splendid view, which had formerly been a Coast Guard post ("Le Corps du Garde"). His wife was nervous about such temerity until the door opened and "a smiling peasant woman" (named Anastasia) greeted them: "Welcome, Monsieur," she said, "I've been expecting you." They adopted "Dream Haven" as their summer home and acquired a Breton spaniel named Coco, a Canadian canoe named Daisy, and their first automobile, a Sigma, an open two-seater, "long and low with graceful lines, and finished in brass that gleamed like gold." It was there in August 1914 that Service heard about the beginning of the Great War: the tocsin rang from the church bells of Lancieux and the mobilization announcement was read in the village square.

*Germaine Service*

"Dream Haven," Lancieux, Brittany. "A little red-roofed house that stood on a sea-jutting rock." *Harper of Heaven*

He tried to join the Seaforth Highlanders, but was refused, not because he was over military age, but because he had a varicose vein in one of his legs. He consulted his friend John Buchan, then a colonel and an M.P., later Lord Tweedsmuir, Governor-General of Canada. They went to a Burns banquet together.

In *Harper of Heaven*[11] and *Rhymes of a Red Cross Man,* there are records of Service's experiences during the first two years of the war. He began as a war correspondent. While trying to get near scenes of action at Dunkirk, he was arrested as a spy. He returned to Paris and was there when the battle of the Marne threatened the city. The first of a series of his articles on the war appeared in the *Toronto Star* on December 11th, 1915: it was entitled "The Hill of Hundred Horrors." In every Saturday issue of the *Star* until January 29th, 1916, there was another instalment: "The Red Harvest," "The Orchestra of War," "Where Ruin Reigns," "The Valley of the Thousand Dead," "In the Trenches," "The Attack," and "On the Inferno's Edge." These descriptions were later worked into a few chapters of *Harper of Heaven.*

His point of view was that of an ambulance driver determined to get as close as possible to the front lines. When an Ambulance Corps was organized in Paris by a group of young Americans "who talked with an Oxford accent and wore handkerchiefs in their sleeves," Service joined them and was soon driving an ambulance and carrying a stretcher under fire. The unit, and Service himself, did good work, and he found satisfaction in the comradeship and in the opportunities for aiding the suffering soldiers.

Before the United States entered the war and the American members of the Red Cross unit

joined their own army, Service was laid low by a
plague of boils. In the course of eight months he
had ninety-nine of them, and was forced to retire
to his home in Paris, and then to his summer place
in Brittany. He decided to spend his time in put-
ting on paper his vivid memories of the front. "I
was due again," he said, "to do a book of rhyme
and here was my material hot to hand. As I had
grabbed my stuff from the Yukon now I would
make the War my meat. . . . Ideas for story poems
came surging at me—the man with no legs, the
man with no arms, the blind man, the faceless
man—all seemed capable of treatment in verse." In
five months he had over sixty poems for *Rhymes of a
Red Cross Man*, which he posted to Fisher Unwin in
London. "The American publishers were enthu-
siastic . . . for nine months [he] headed the list of
best sellers in the *Bookman*."

To the poet's experiences as a stretcher-bearer
one may attribute the manifest seriousness of the
mood in which he reported the war with a mini-
mum of propaganda or rhetorical exaggeration.
The conflict was only half over, but it had clearly
become a matter of trench warfare. Readers now
under fifty years of age who have become acquainted with "World War I" largely through photographs and bits of documentary films may find
their cool responses heated up even now by the
hard, explicit details, the common sentiments, and
the contrasting grim humour in these verses of Service; for old-timers there is nostalgia, pain, and
vivid memories.

These rhymes display little jingoism, but much
disillusionment, and much compassion. The book
is not about the politics, the concerns of power
blocs, the general campaigns, and not even about
the officer class. It is about the individual soldiers,

mainly British privates and some German victims, each one on the "common" level. It is the "Trail" all over again in its deliberate facing of danger and even more imminent death, but its romantic impulses are inspired by loyalty, not by greed. The mood of the ballads and the "scraps of song" is like that of Burns, rather than that of Kipling or Henley—certainly uncoloured by refinement such as that of Rupert Brooke or John McCrae.

Most of the poems make a direct appeal to the reader in the form of monologues and in language approximating the actual speech (the slang and the catch-words) of the fighting men (mainly cockneys named Bill) and of their loved ones back home. The ambulance man does not adopt a superior or detached attitude, for he has shared all but the worst of the horrors of trench warfare. In this book we have vivid sensations of soldiers marching gaily up to the front; the first experiences of shelling and bombing; qualms of anxiety about "doing one's bit;" the waiting for a signal to "go over the top" into No Man's Land; the excitement of the attack, the barbed-wire, the mud, and the hail of bullets; the machine gun trap; the corpses; crawling from hole to hole; the sudden fall of buddies; the inhumanity of hand-to-hand slaughter; the sense of futility about a gain of a few yards; the resolute acceptance of temporary safety or of personal disaster; sometimes oblivion or the horror of missing limbs; dressing stations; death for many; the pride and desolation of mothers and fathers; the overriding goal, not so much victory, as peace.

This is not a series of verses from which one picks out favourite word-pictures; the book has a single focus on the precarious life of a common soldier. Service does not attempt to summarize the events of the war and their significance. In that

Robert Service in uniform, 1916. *Germaine Service*

year of 1916 he could only say, with his "Stretcher-Bearer":[12]

> *Look! like a ball of blood the sun*
> *'Angs o'er the scene of wrath and wrong—*
> *Quick! Stretcher-bearers on the run!*
> *O Prince of Peace! 'ow long, 'ow long?*

He dedicated *The Rhymes of a Red Cross Man* "to the Memory of *My Brother*, Lieutenant Albert Service, Canadian Infantry, Killed in Action, France, August 1916."

While the book was being widely read, Service got back to the war on an assignment from the Canadian government to report activities of the Canadian Expeditionary Force. Having the amenities of an officer—"a Cadillac, a chauffeur, an officer guide and freedom to choose and plan [his] itinerary" he saw a great deal more of what went on behind the whole front. He was attached first to the Foresters and then to the Engineers. One of the camps of the Labour Battalions was commanded by an old friend, James Cornwall, whom he had met at Athabaska Landing on his trip to the Yukon by way of the Mackenzie.[13] He had described Cornwall as "Peace River Jim", one of "the great men of the North." This officer took Service to see "one of the hottest spots of the battle ground," where the retreating Germans were still pouring shells into Belgian towns. There was danger and desolation: corpses, heaps of rubble, barbed wire, mines, and pathetic scenes too numerous to write about at the time, even in notes for prose articles.

Service's final exposure to the war was a triumph of good luck and mischief. In a car with a Canadian major, he found himself in the coal mining area around Denain, "farther than any British troops had yet penetrated." They pushed on toward Lille and, passing through cheering crowds, entered that city by the Cambrai gate just as the Germans were leaving on the other side. They received the welcome and kisses of conquerors!

Service was in Paris and witnessed the mob scenes of victory. For several months he had been in the city, working hard on a book of prose to be called *War Winners*. He had turned out article after article, "describing saw-mills, hospitals, bakeries, ordnance camps—all the organization that makes fighting possible. [He] gave the names of hundreds of those 'who also serve,' and said something interesting about each." So the book had grown. *War Winners* "would deal with the efforts of those who worked without glory to win glory for others." Victory, however, brought him only thoughts of those who had died for it: he tore up his manuscript, and joined his wife at "Dream Haven" in Brittany.

The post-war phase began in 1918 or 1919 when the apartment in Paris became too small for the family's requirements and for their bank account. They found a magnificent residence on the Place du Pantheon, "*bourgeois* in its gaudy splendour": an apartment offering ten times the amount of space belonging to the "Hutch," including a studio which Robert made into a library lined with a thousand books. This would be their home for the next ten years.

Service now played a role which he considered appropriate for a famous author living in "princely" luxury in such a pretentious neighbourhood. His old friend Peter McQuattie, who had risen to the position of manager of a Paris news agency, incited him to wear a monocle and to buy his suits at the best tailors. Concealing his inferiority, he said, he looked superciliously at the world and was adorned in "sartorial splendour."

*Germaine Service*

Place du Pantheon, Paris, 1919-1929. The Services' apartment on the sixth floor with studio and terrace on the seventh floor offered a splendid view across Paris.

His investments doubled and he was "in danger of becoming a millionaire, a fate [he] would not have wished on [his] worst enemy." Business affairs bored him, and, as his stock continued to go up, he still professed the superior contentment of poverty. When a crash came after several years of booming prices, he lost a good deal, but he sold his bank stock and bought a large life annuity from an insurance company.

During the first year after the war, he worked at "Dream Haven" on his fifth book of verse which would eventually bear the title of *Ballads of a Bohemian*. He was still experimenting:

> *It dealt with the Latin Quarter, the War,*
> *Brittany, and because it was the most*
> *autobiographical of my verse I dislike it least.*
> *In it I tried the device of linking up the poems*
> *with patches of prose, making a connected story*
> *of the whole. I like the prose better than the*
> *verse and still think a few words of*
> *commentary enhances its interest.*

This book purported to be the work of Stephen Poore, an American bohemian poet who lived in Montparnasse before the war; served in the Ambulance-Corps; was wounded at Verdun; left the Corps in the spring of 1917 to join the United States Army in France; lost his left arm in the Argonne; and was still in the American hospital at Neuilly in January 1919.[14]

If this book of Service's—in spite of the usual literary mask—is autobiographical and a kind of summary of his Parisian and war years from 1913 to 1919, one must notice that it leaves out all aspects of his married life but concentrates on observations made as a bohemian bachelor, as a writer deliberately studying the life of the Latin Quarter, or as an ambulance man.

This book is unusual not only in displaying "patches of prose" to link the ballads, but it also has a curious seasonal arrangement ranging over the years 1914 to 1919. The first part, "Spring" is set in Montparnasse in April and May 1914, when the poet is represented as living in poverty in a garret. The second part, "Early Summer" (June 1914) identifies some ballads with parks (Montsouris and the Luxembourg) and cafés (the Deux Magots and the Closerie des Lilas). The third part, "Late Summer" finds the poet in the Omnium Bar, the Café du Dôme, the Garden of the Luxembourg, the Café de la Source and the Café de la Paix (late in July 1914), and in Brittany in August, when the war begins. In the fourth part, "Winter," the poet is with the Ambulance Corps on the Somme Front and in Picardy (January 1915) and near Albert (February 1915). The last part, with this heading, "A lapse of time and a word of explanation," quotes Stephen Poore's letter of January 1919 and the advertisement for copies of his book to be sent out to subscribers from the Rue des Petits Moineaux in Paris.

*Ballads of a Bohemian* was written in a mood of compassion for the poor and unfortunate people of the Quarter as well as for the mutilated, dying, and bereaved in the war. The grim comedy of the Sourdough period and the artful objectivity of *The Pretender* had given way to the warm human fellowship of these ballads, and the author was not yet taking personal refuge in natural beauty as he would do when he exploited in his novels the cinematic ironies of vice and crime.

The dominant image of the "Spring" section is the moon, which turns the magic city into a dream, and evokes the poet's fancies. The setting is his own garret, or the boulevards and the cafés where all

kinds of people pass by. He takes them home in his
mind, and he becomes the characters about whom
he writes.

*Stories, stories jump at me.*
*Moving tales my pen might write;*
*Poems plain on every face;*
*Monologues you could recite*
*With inimitable grace.*

His "grace" was rarely "inimitable," but he was a
sensitive and conscientious poet, always ready to
experiment within the limits of his professed purpose: he said of "The Wee Shop" that "its theme is
commonplace, its language that of everyday. It is a
bit of realism in rhyme." There was always rhyme,
and the line lengths varied from poem to poem,
evidently in response to moods and the pauses of
speech; there are short lines like "Up the old Boul'
Mich'," and long ones like "You've heard of Julot
the *apache,* and Gigolette, his môme. . . ." In this
month of May he sang the joy of little things, for
carnival was king in Paris then—in spite of clouds
and before the breaking of the storm.

In "Early Summer" there is more strain upon
the freedom which is supposed to redeem poverty,
failure, "Hunger and Thirst and Cold." To his gallery of those who were lost in this endeavour, Service added the widow and the lame girl of "The
Wee Shop"; the painter who had to become a "Pencil Seller"; Marie Toro, fallen queen of the Carnival; a despairing "Painter Chap"; a "Little Work-
girl"; a worn-out concert singer; and the
"Coco-Fiend."

*Fête in Brittany* was the title of a "brave big picture" painted by the "Pencil Seller." In the section
of *Ballads* entitled "Late Summer," the poet also re-
sponds to Brittany, and he sets out from Paris—no
longer in tune with the city—for the "Land of Little

Fields." Before leaving the boulevards, he affirms rather wistfully the delights of bohemian freedom, especially for the young, and the inevitability of romance becoming an exercise for the easy chair. But he still walks the streets, especially along the Quays "between the leafage and the sunlit Seine." He is very fond of "the stealing in of night." Yet he feels too healthy to be stifled where there are no great open spaces. "With staff and scrip" he sees himself footing it in Finistère—another land of dreams. The prose now becomes lyrical as he stays by the sea with his friend Calvert and approaches "Dream Haven." There he hears about the war.

The descriptions and anecdotes of "Winter" are supplements to *The Rhymes of a Red Cross Man*: the rather similar ballads of the last section of the *Bohemian* book are devoted to the still suffering survivors of the war, such as "The Sightless Man," "The Legless Man," and "The Faceless Man." Service had found that he could tear up the manuscript of his projected book of War Winners, but he could not forget what others still endured. He finished the manuscript for the *Ballads* at Dream Haven before joining his wife for Christmas in 1919 in Paris. In a reaction to emotional stress and overwork, he allowed the book to lie neglected for more than a year. *Ballads of a Bohemian* was not published until Barse and Hopkins brought it out in New York in 1921.

The literary movements of high artistic quality which he saw being born in Paris at this time were not for him. He was, however, not without knowledge of some of the fashionable currents in art and literature. In an amusing series of couplets entitled "The Philistine and the Bohemian,"[15] he presents the bohemian man in "a cape and brigand hat" speaking about Mallarmé and Paul Verlaine, "Vorticist's suppers," Strauss and Stravinski. The "Philistine," a girl, affects conservative elegance rather than art until she changes into a "consummate Bohemian," "dressed like the dames of Rossetti and E. Burne Jones," and chattering about Bergson, Pater's prose, Matisse, Cézanne, Tschaikovsky, and César Franck, and gushing over "some weirdly Futurist daub." Meanwhile, the man has become a "simpering dandy," who talks about dances and ragtime shows, the girls of Kirchner, and jazz bands. "He thought her a bore, she thought him an ass."

> *And what is the moral of all this rot?*
> *Don't try to be what you know you're not.*
> *And if you're made on a muttonish plan,*
> *Don't seek to seem a Bohemian;*
> *And if to the goats your feet incline,*
> *Don't try to pass for a Philistine.*

Service knew Gertrude Stein by sight and would gladly have acquired her little house on the rue de Fleurus. The familiar story of other British and American expatriates will be recalled by this passage in *Harper of Heaven*:

> *In the Quarter small magazines were being*
> *produced, each with its mission of modernity.*
> *Blocking the doorway of Silvia Beach's*
> *Bookshop one could see the portly form of Ford*
> *Madox Ford, accompanied by the vivacious*
> *Violet Hunt. In the shop with its*
> *Shakespearean sign one would run into James*
> *Joyce peering short-sightedly at the shelves, or*
> *Antheil the composer buzzing with enthusiasm.*
> *In the Quarter were many who afterwards*
> *became famous—Giants in Gestation.*

Henry Miller, whom he met by chance, advised him to keep his eyes "on a man called Hemingway."

If Service and Hemingway met during the early 1920s, they had plenty of topics for conversation in spite of differences in temperament and literary views. Both men were interested in outdoor life, in boxing, and in physical fitness. Both of them had been ambulance drivers: Service in France in 1914-15, Hemingway in Italy in 1918, where he had been wounded by a trench mortar. Indeed, the information given by Charles A. Fenton (in *The Apprenticeship of Ernest Hemingway*)[16] about the American Volunteer Motor-Ambulance Corps in France, founded by Richard Norton of Boston in 1914 and consisting largely of college men, strongly suggests the very unit with which Service was associated until the United States entered the war; Hemingway belonged to the successor to this corps which served in Italy under the Red Cross. During 1920 and 1921 Hemingway was employed in Toronto; when he returned to Paris at the end of 1921, Service had gone to spend the winter in Hollywood.

It is doubtful that Service ever thought of breaking into the circle of contributors to the *Little Review* or Ford Madox Ford's *transatlantic review*; he was still intent on going his own way, and now striving to be "modern" in the sense of contemporary, on the level of the slicks and the movies. He greeted with enthusiasm a cheque from a Hollywood producer in the amount of five thousand dollars for the picture rights of "one of [his] books." It is probable that he was referring to the first moving picture to be made of his work—not of a book, however, but of a poem, "The Shooting of Dan McGrew."[17]

The excitement produced by this promise of success in filmland prompted Service to take his wife and their little daughter Iris to Hollywood. His mother, coming south from Alberta, would spend the winter of 1921-22 with them. Robert had not seen his mother for ten years—she was now a jolly woman in her seventies, eager to fit into their pleasant household and to enjoy the delights of the moving picture city.

Los Angeles was greatly changed since he had seen it twenty years earlier: it had become a "magic Land of Make Believe." On his first day in Hollywood, he saw Charlie Chaplin and Lila Lee, and rented a hillside bungalow, belonging to Carrie Jacobs Bond, for a period of six months. The whole visit to Hollywood followed this pattern of watching the "stars" and enjoying a leisurely domestic life. Movies were frequently being shot in public view on the streets of Hollywood; meetings with such producers as Selig Seligman, Louis Mayer, and Robert Hughes could be arranged. Service met, and was photographed with, Marie Prevost, Priscilla Dean, William "Big Bill" Russell, and other actors. In a kind of summary, Service wrote: "We ate lunch in the Sunset Cafeteria on the Boulevard—in my case usually hamburger and apple pie—but we had supper at home by a roaring fire." This kind of life pleased his mother. "Her diversions," he said, "were cards and crime; the first in the form of solitaire, the second, . . . gangster films, dime novels, and banana ice-cream."

During that winter of 1921-22, cinema audiences saw such films as Charlie Chaplin's *The Kid,* Ibàñez's *The Four Horsemen of the Apocalypse,* and Robert J. Flaherty's *Nanook of the North,* but there were also "westerns," and a few stories of mystery, wickedness, and madness. Several films, *Godless Men, The Lotus Eater* (with John Barrymore), and *Moran of the Lady Letty* (with Rudolph Valentino) employed scenes of waterfronts, oceans, and islands in the Pacific. There was a great deal of violence and melodrama.

On Service's return from a sidetrip to Tahiti,

he joined his family in Hollywood and engaged in a strenuous "fight with fat," to lose twenty-five pounds. He was fit and ready for work when, in 1922, his mother left for Canada and he, his wife, and little Iris returned to the "princely apartment" near the Pantheon. On the terrace he could look at the "raking roofs of the Sorbonne, the sparkle of the Seine and the serried heights of Montmartre." He was now a man of considerable sophistication and self-acquired breadth of knowledge of literature. He had long been what is called "an omnivorous reader" and he now had a personal library of English and French literary masterpieces. There and at "Dream Haven" he prepared his own contributions to Hollywood's stock of thrillers.

The first of these, a movie entitled *The Shooting of Dan McGrew*, released in 1924, required no preparation on his part; Hollywood made its own melodrama based on his famous poem.[18] It was directed by Clarence Badger, and featured Lew Cody as Dan McGrew, Barbara La Marr as the lady known as Lou, and Percy Marmont as the piano-playing Stranger. When the film arrived at the Capitol in New York in June 1924 it was accompanied by a "pot-pourri" of Victor Herbert melodies. The production was panned by the *Times'* reviewer. He found it "tame," "amateurish": the picture was set, at the beginning, in the South Seas, then in New York, and so to the Yukon. There was little suggestion of the cold North. The picture was not saved by beautiful Miss La Marr. The reviewer found her unimpressive in this film. "Her overdoctored lips glisten in the glare of the Kleig lights, and she indulges in her usual conception of excitement by panting."

The second of his Hollywood thrillers, *Poisoned Paradise*, was more effectively based upon his

Culver Pictures

A scene from the Hollywood film *The Shooting of Dan McGrew*, 1924. "A bunch of the boys were whooping it up in the Malamute saloon."

Germaine Service

Robert Service and Marlene Dietrich in costume for their roles in *The Spoilers*, Hollywood, 1942.

second European novel, *The Poisoned Paradise,* published in 1922. It was a literary product of journeys which he made before and after marriage, but principally during a few post-war years, especially after he acquired a motor car.

There is a good deal of specialized knowledge about gambling in *The Poisoned Paradise.* Merely to write such a book, the author had to be acquainted with dangerous lore about systems designed to beat the roulette wheel and to break the bank. He may have had his initiation in this art at Whitehorse or Dawson, although he must have practised it in prudent moderation. It is certain that he had indulged modestly in this game at Dinard, near St. Malo, when he was "Baedekering in Brittany" in 1912 or 1913, for, in the *Toronto Star* of January 3rd, 1914, he told how he had risked thirty francs a day successfully according to a system of his own invention. Whether he played a bit more on unrecorded visits to Monte Carlo is not known. In his romance, he displayed knowledge of the game so thorough and technical that some detailed expositions have to be skipped by unpractised readers.

The love story which holds *The Poisoned Paradise* together is related, in Service's characteristic fashion, with few scenes of passionate embraces but many details enthralling an observer. Margot, the heroine, sees in a portrait of herself

> *these curves of milky shoulders, that slim, silky*
> *beauty of neck and throat, the shell-like ear,*
> *the faintly hollow cheek with its suggestion of*
> *pathetic sweetness, and above all the superb*
> *mass of hair—here glinting with the brightness*
> *of stubble in September sunshine, there richly*
> *gold as the ripened grain.*

Margot spent her early years in Parisian scenes

most familiar to Service before his Pantheon
period: she was the poor girl of romance who had
to spend her youth at work in various shops.

The ancestors of the hero—as romance requires—had been rich and proud: Hugh's mother
was a poor, neglected widow. While very young, he
was cared for in London by a Mr. and Mrs. Ainger
who lived in Balmoral Circus. Later he got a job,
served in France during the war, and was sent to
the Riviera for his health.

On the train to the south he met his first roulette advisers, one of whom was the alluring Mrs.
Belmire, who wished to teach him more than gambling. Hugh left the train at Monaco, along with his
new-found acquaintances, and became familiar
with a city upon which he (an amateur painter) and
Service (his fictional biographer) lavished affection
and indignation.

Hugh saw Margot on the train: she "looked interesting." Their next meeting is sensational, for
she is caught seizing his pocketbook. She has fallen
so low because she is starving. They decide upon an
unusual solution—which, incidentally, Sir Pelham
Pelham, the old Casanova, told Service had failed
happily for himself and a countess.[19] Hugh and
Margot make a pact to observe a chaste brother-
sister arrangement as they share a small apartment.
The plan works too well for romance because
Hugh spends nearly all his time at the Casino,
learning gambling systems and playing the wheel
with the excuses of making just enough money to
pay expenses, to send Margot back to Paris, to buy
himself a motor car, and to acquire a cottage near
Villefranche. He also becomes more deeply involved in Mrs. Belmire's greedy possessiveness and
in protection of the infallible winning system of an
old professor. From this point in the book, Hugh

finds himself a captive of ruffians planning to rob
the Casino. At the same time, the Casino police
make him an unwilling agent of their own designs.

When Margot returns to Paris, Hugh goes on a
trip to Corsica, where the ruffians turn up again
and chase him all over the countryside in mo-
torized gangster style, for he has inadvertently
come into possession of their loot. Of course he
escapes, finds Margot in Paris, marries her, sup-
ports her on an unexpected legacy from his mater-
nal grandmother, and rejoices in a son and heir.
They live in paradise, exempt from its poison.

Sometimes the story appears to be an excuse
for writing a travelogue. Hugh is given a trip to
Corsica, probably because Robert and Germaine
Service had made two trips to this French island in
the Mediterranean after the war.[20] Such things as
arrivals and first impressions, lodgings and food,
characters living close to nature, and scenery itself—especially rough scenery—fascinated Service.
Hugh had his first view when,[21]

> In the glimmer of early dawn, the big boat
> swung slowly into the harbour. Under the
> lightening sky the steel grey waters changed to
> steel blue; and the dark mysterious land smiled
> into friendliness. The grey cubes piled against
> the mountain brightened into tall houses still
> locked in sleep. Presently, with a fore-glow of
> citron, the clear rim of the sun cut the sea-line;
> and the sea became jade green. The air was
> diamond pure; the mountains took on colour;
> and Bastia awakened to another careless day.
> High caserne-like houses, massive-walled
> and stucco-fronted; shabby shops half a
> century behind the times; mustiness and age;
> cigarettes, vendetta knives, and
> goat-flesh,—these were some of Hugh's first
> impressions of Bastia.

In the course of Hugh's adventures, there are
descriptions of the valley of the Golo, the kindly
people, the statuesque shepherds, the grey villages,
and the pines of the mountains. In other parts of
the book, there is evidence of more rapturous delight in the southern coast of France, the Riviera.[22]

> *The scenery was as lovely as a painted panel.*
> *Between umbrella pines he saw the majestic*
> *sway of the sea. Snowy villas peeped from*
> *sombre cyprus groves. The palms were pale*
> *gold in the wistful sunshine. Magic names*
> *glorified the common-place looking*
> *stations.—San Raphael, Agay, Nice. In the*
> *setting sun the way seemed to be growing more*
> *and more wonderful, as if working up to a*
> *climax of beauty. . . . And to think that this*
> *loveliness had been here all the time, and he*
> *had not known!*

*Poisoned Paradise* was filmed in Hollywood
under the direction of L. Gasnier. Kenneth Harlan
played the part of Hugh, the famous Clara Bow
took the part of Margot, and Carmel Myers that of
Mrs. Belmire. This production followed Service's
story quite closely. A reviewer of films for the *New
York Times* of August 11th, 1924, thought that *The
Poisoned Paradise* deserved something better than a
"dime-novel title."[23] He found in it "a great deal of
truth interspersed with impossible fiction," and he
regretted that the director had not made it a more
important picture with "a little more study" of
Monte Carlo and "the existence there":

> *He could have shown the losers applying for*
> *enough money to return home, the men who*
> *were saved from misfortune by having a train*
> *to catch at the height of their good luck, the*
> *women who faint and vanish through mirrored*
> *doors and the old women who beg for money in*
> *the perfumed atmosphere of the roulette room.*

# 7 Tales of
# Evil in
# Paradise

*The Poisoned Paradise* was a financial and cinematic
success; it gave Service a pattern. He had felt unable to oblige his mother when she begged for detective stories "because the cold logic of them"
bored him. But he could make up "stories that
leaped from one lurid situation to another." His
imagination was flamboyant, and it was easy for
him to provide more thrillers.[1]

There was no problem in finding additional
settings for romances: Paris, Tahiti and Moorea,
and Brittany were also, in many ways, earthly para-
dises of his own experience and his fancy. Yet none
of these Edens was free of crime, and fictional con-
trasts between good and evil could yield irony and
melodrama. With a deep sense of human vulnera-
bility, he exploited the plight of his Adams and
Eves under the attacks of dehumanized monsters.

Since his mother had specified stories about
gangsters, he was determined to learn all that he
could about the Parisian "substitute," the *apache*, in

the slumland at his very door. Following an old habit, however, he allowed the material accumulating in his Parisian notebook to cool off before he used it for fiction. His sense of place and personal involvement was, at first, too strong for contrivances of plotting and characterization, and, until his fancy had time to develop a fictional plan, he turned to something else.

In 1922 he went back to his notebook on Tahiti, a goal of his youth achieved on a sidetrip away from Hollywood. The ambition to go to this dreamland had been inspired by Robert Louis Stevenson's *In the South Seas* (1900), and he had whetted his appetite for beachcombing by reading *White Shadows in the South Seas* (1920) by Frederick O'Brien. During the voyage on the *Raratonga* bound for Tahiti, he had reread Stevenson, O'Brien, and Charles Warren Stoddard (author of *South Sea Idylls*). In addition, he had such current books as Hall and Nordhoff's *Faery Lands of the South Seas* (1921) and Somerset Maugham's *The Moon and Sixpence* (1919), a story which Maugham acknowledged, on his first page, "was suggested by the life of Paul Gaugin," the painter who was in Tahiti and the Marquesas during the 1890s. In Tahiti, Service was destined to meet the men who would later achieve fame for the story of the *Bounty*: Charles Bernard Nordhoff ("a handsome young fellow, blond and brimming with vitality") and James Norman Hall, then in hospital. He saw Hall as "long, lean, dark . . . of the Stevenson type [who] would have made a grand Scotsman."

For two months Service had made notes of all he saw and he had acquired all the descriptive material which he needed for *The Roughneck*. The nature of these notes may be learned from the first person reports later published in three vivid chapters of *Harper of Heaven*, entitled "Beach-comber De Luxe," "Tramping Round Tahiti," and "Moorean Idyll."[2]

His choice of a story leaping from one lurid situation to another may have been, in the long run, a mistake. Had he addressed himself fully to the business of being a travel writer, and published his descriptions and anecdotes in a separate Tahiti book, he might have established himself in that category as a rival of the authors whom he had so recently read. His strength lay in rhetorical description of this paradise.

The plot of *The Roughneck*, indeed, appears to have been invented as a framework for descriptive passages. The novel was written over a period of nine months at "Dream Haven." Years later, in *Harper of Heaven*, he called it "a series of dramatic situations linked up to form a story." No better definition of it could be given than his own: "when the hero was not rescuing the heroine from dire peril the heroine was saving the hero from imminent disaster."[3]

The hero, who suffered at the hands of a succession of villains, was named Jerry Delane. He had been left penniless as a child, because his father had been cheated by "Stealwell Austin" in a business partnership. Jerry, as a boy working in the Orion Safe Works, was "framed" by "Skeeter Simms," and sent to the penitentiary for theft. When he came out, he became a "bruiser," a boxer, albeit a "Hamlet of the Ring," taken on a tour by his manager to Australia. En route, he spent a day at Papeete (on Tahiti). His fight with "Tiger Morissy" in Paris upon his return to Europe was described in great detail by Service, who was at this time on his "physical culture" campaign.

Jerry's arm was broken, and he gave up the

ring to return to America. On the way, he decided, to visit the home of his ancestors (where but in Brittany?) and his mother, old, blind, and poverty-stricken. Here he met his mother's friend, Felicity, a rich and attractive girl who would reappear throughout the novel and arouse bitter-sweet and hopeless affection on Jerry's part. Felicity's beauty and the scenic charms of Tahiti and Moorea bring a measure of relief to a thriller which features encounters with human "snakes" in that South Seas garden.

Service contrived to move Jerry to Papeete as an exile after an apparently fatal assault upon his father's persecutor, the millionaire Austin; Felicity turned up on Tahiti because she owned a large plantation on the neighbouring island of Moorea. The physically superb beachcomber and the young lady meet in Papeete, but they are at odds because of Jerry's stubborn silence and the vast difference in their fortunes and social positions. The circumstances which bring them briefly together are recorded as a long series of melodramatic escapes from villains on various parts of the islands which Service himself had visited.

Some of the bad guys whom he was offering his readers and the studios of Hollywood bore the names of Hyacinthe Beauregard, Marc Macara (a "gorilla"), little Smeet, gross Gunsburg, Dirty Hank, amorous Windy Bill, Gridley, Simms, and Captain Barbazo. Violence, intrigue, surprise, hair's-breadth escapes, the macabre, and the mysterious, are exploited beyond credibility. The plot is unravelled by the reappearance of "Skeeter Simms", formerly of the Orion Safe Works in the United States.

Service had only the resources of language to describe what Gaugin had made immortal in paint, but he did his extravagant best in presenting the variety of scenes on the islands. This is how he competed with the other travellers in picturing an arrival at Papeete:[4]

> *Then from the roaring whiteness of the reef*
> *they turned to look at the land.*
> *It seemed to leap at them in the eager*
> *appeal of its beauty. Through the crystal*
> *clearness the velvety shores were radiant with*
> *joy and color. Those pale groves must be*
> *coconut palms. Down to the beach they*
> *thronged, leaning over the water and*
> *fluttering a frivolous welcome. Behind them*
> *were tenebrous mountains matted with jungle.*
> *It was a steep land, smothered in greenery. Its*
> *violent verdure cataracted down the flanks of*
> *the hills, and petered out in those pale*
> *flirtatious palms.*

Everywhere in the book one sees such evidence of Service the enthusiast and amateur painter, enjoying the most incidental details, such as merely crossing a stream:[5] "There were good-sized pools and the water had an opal tint, like soapy water. In the depths were giant black shrimps. The rocks were covered with russet-colored lizards, and mosquitoes rose in clouds. How fortunate there were no snakes."

Years later, when he wrote *Harper of Heaven,* he drew upon his notes and the pages of his *Roughneck* for descriptions of his own beachcombing observations in Tahiti and Moorea. The exact words of the passage about pools reappear in *Harper.* Among his adventures was entertainment by a local chief at a feast where he sat "like a young faun" surrounded by nymphs: "Ah, those golden girls! Their hair spun out like clouds of night starred

with flowers, their velvety eyes voluptuously shin-
ing, their brown breasts like ripe pomegranates . . .
Oh boy! I thought, it's time for you to hike back to
the domestic hearth." He went back to his family
with considerable doubt about the ultimate satisfaction of a primitive state of existence, and with in-
creased compassion for the state of the poor and
distressed on both sides of the world.

*The Roughneck* was published in 1922 by Barse
and Hopkins of New York and received its first
showing as a Hollywood film late in 1924. The
moving picture featured George O'Brien as Jerry
Delane, and Billy Dove as Felicity. The *motifs* were
largely retained in spite of a radical transformation
of incidents. A few examples will suffice: Jerry's
mother appears, not in Brittany, but on the South
Sea island, and, in a featured scene, Jerry is rescued by a native girl when he is fighting under
water with a shark. A reviewer in the *New York
Times* (December 3rd, 1924)[6] gave special attention
to the physique of George O'Brien—deep chest,
brawny arms, "the strength of an ox," "the ankles
of a Mercury," and "an artistic waist line,"—a
model of Service's own ideal of physical perfection.
The reviewer thought the film to be "a boy's idea of
adventure."

Between 1923 and 1926 there was a gap in the
publication of Service's series of thrillers, and between 1924 and 1928 another gap in the filming of
his work. An explanation for this apparent silence
was given in his most unusual book entitled *Why
Not Grow Young? Or Living For Longevity*. It was a
handbook on exercise, diet, and hygiene for men
who had reached fifty (Service's age in 1924). His
literary enterprise had taken a temporary detour.
The book, however, may be read as a tale of evil in
a paradise—the evil being Service's cardiac trouble
and the Eden being Royat in the French moun-

tains. The vulnerable hero at long last was explicitly Service himself, and this was his first work of autobiography.

His heart trouble derived in part from his Tahitian experience, for the men he saw there impressed him with their physical perfection while he daily ate too much and put on weight. In Hollywood and Paris, therefore, he resorted to some of the currently fashionable programmes of physical culture, to reduce fat, expand his chest muscles, and make himself "like a picture postcard of Gene Tunney." His exercises, carried to a ridiculous extreme, first spasmodic, then systematic, then passionate, were too much for a man approaching fifty. Alas, he could not develop his male form like "the gold and tawny men [of Tahiti] girt in gold and scarlet loin-cloths [who] lolled under the flame trees with the grace of gods [or] among the palm groves. . . . [They] stalked with the majesty of kings."[7] He attributed "the temporary bad behaviour" of his heart to three causes: "too rapid reduction of weight, heavy dumb-bells in exercise, and excessive Turkish bathing."

What the doctors said shocked him into a programme for a cure. He had to give up all harmful habits and put himself under the care of Professor Gabriel Perrin of Clermont University at "the magical springs" of Royat in Auvergne. Characteristically, he entered fully into his doctor's routine and learned the technical details of treatment. During three seasons at Royat, he revelled in luxurious baths, blissful rests between the sheets, and long walks up the hills and down into the green valley— all designed to reduce his blood pressure. The deprivations were much harder to accept: "alcohol, tobacco, red meat, coffee and every form of exciting food" were wholly or drastically banned.

The handbook which emerged from this or-

deal opened with an autobiographical section
going back to the days of his youth and early man-
hood: his boyish fondness for solitary walking or
reading of books, his ambition to go to sea, his lack
of nerve as a "Casanova," his wanderlust, his bondage as a wage-slave, his perfect health and moderation in the Yukon, his love of nature, and his de-
cline into bad habits of overeating as a result of
prosperity.

After more than a hundred pages containing a
merciless, sardonic catalogue of do's and dont's,
presented first as homilies and then as summed-up
memoranda—mercifully omitted here—Service
closed his book with a chapter on "The Religion of
A Man of Fifty." His working philosophy as a
"Plain Man" was addressed to "the Philosopher in
Every Man" and was identified as practical and ma-
terialistic:

*I realize that I am a fool and that I know
nothing. But I do not see that others are much
wiser or know a great deal more. Baffled by
the mystery that surrounds me, I cease to puzzle
over it. Having satisfied my lust for reality I
am willing to return to illusion again. Unable
to understand life, I accept it as it presents
itself, seeking to get all the enjoyment out of it
I can. Thrown back on life itself in its concrete
and actual presentment I become resigned to a
destiny I cannot fathom. I make the best of my
circumstances, try to put myself in harmony
with them. I develop my capacity for the
enjoyment of surface values such as form and
colour; I accept emotions and sentiments at
their face value. I cease trying to probe the
depths, and without question take my happiness
as it comes. . . . As to the existence of a God, I
know nothing. But I maintain that nobody*

*does know anything. And this is just as it
should be, for whatever the nature of supreme
reality, it is inconceivable that it should be
conceivable. . . . Kindness and sympathy is the
best religion of all.*

In this way *Why Not Grow Young?* set forth the
ideals, routines, and attitudes repeated in the more
didactic verse which Service wrote during his later
life. It reflected, of course, the active programme
he followed during the period of convalescence
(1924-1926), when there were three annual visits to
Royat, along with summers of leisure at Dream
Haven and winters in an apartment on the Riviera
at Nice. Most of the book was written in a "halycon"
month of midsummer in Brittany, probably as
early as 1926.

When the publishers, Ernest Benn of London,
eventually (in 1928) brought out this untypical
work of the Yukon poet, the frontispiece was a picture of "the writer wearing the costume [bathing
trunks] in which he wrote this book." The photo-
graph was taken from the side to show his loss of
fat—a silhouette of a lean man able to hold in his
middle. With such encouragement, men of fifty
can still read *Why Not Grow Young?* with profit if not
delight, and, unless they keep their copies well hid-
den, their physicians, dietitians, and wives may in-
sist upon its constant use.

Service's leisurely programme for recovery did
not exclude the use of his mind and pen. *The Master
of the Microbe*, his second last thriller, was produced
during this period. It may have been partially written as early as 1922-23 on the basis of that bulky
notebook about slumland which he had set aside in
order to concentrate on the Tahiti material.

Once more he wove a series of dramatic scenes
around descriptive passages from his notes. If one

compares chapters sixteen to eighteen of *Harper of Heaven* with *The Master of the Microbe,* Service's practice of merging his own observations with a framework of fiction becomes very clear. The novel itself presents a report of how and where he conducted his campaign for personal knowledge of the Parisian slumlands.[8] By 1948 (the date of *Harper*), his notebooks of the 1920s may have been lost, but large blocks of description from them had long been preserved, largely word for word, in the novel. In *Harper,* therefore, he quite properly laid claim to these descriptions as the truth about his own experiences during his campaign in the "lower depths."

At first he went alone to the places he described in his books, wearing "a turtle-necked grey sweater, a cloth cap and old flannel trousers," and slouching like an *apache.* Yet, in the Café de Rome, a haunt of cut-throats, a bar-girl spotted him as a *"flic Américain,"* a movie-type detective "after a gangster from Chicago." When great danger threatened, he was happy to accept the protection and connivance of Jean Dulac of the Sûreté. On dropping a hint that he wrote books, he was awarded the respect given to a celebrated poet.[9] Of this he said: "A poet! I realized that here in artistic Paris the word had an honourable meaning for even the least of those policemen and won a respect it would have done nowhere else in the world."

The rue Moufetard, "the juiciest slum in all the city," was not far from Service's Pantheon house. "Near it," he wrote in *Harper of Heaven,* "is the rue St. Medard, frequented by the garbage rakers and close by is the Flea Market, where they sell their finds. Round the Place Maubert radiate poisonous alleys and close by is the Café des Clochards, refuge of those homeless outcasts who sleep under the bridges of the Seine."

In *The Master of the Microbe,* Service was able to present vivid details about the "Au Lapin Vengeur," a *bal musette* near the Belleville gate (pp. 132-144); the Zone, a warren for criminals (170-171 and 241-243); the "Café des Bons Enfants" (296) in the Rue Moufetard; the underground river, the Beivre (301); the dance halls of the Rue de Lappe (188-191) and the Passage Thierry (191-194); the Café des Clochards at the foot of the Rue Dante (215-218); "the Cavern of the Dead" in the Rue de l'Hotel Colbert (218-221); and even about old Colombe, the woman who lived in a sewer-pipe for ten years (222-223). The old chateau and its charnel pit in the forest of Senart (273, 314) may have been merely an invention for further "gothic" effect, but the descriptive power of the Parisian settings gives support to Service's claim that he came to know "the lower depths of Paris as [he believed] no other writer of English knew them."[10]

Down in the slums he saw the living original of Casque d'Or, the golden-haired accordionist and singer who lends charm to *The Master of the Microbe.* In some ways, the hero of the novel, Harley Quin, is a reflection of Service himself, for Quin is drawn into the slumland scenes by a desire to secure documentation for a novel to be entitled *Garbage,* about "a woman doomed from her birth to infamy." The hero's name, readily suggesting "Harlequin," carried one back to Service's *The Pretender,* for a "harlequin" is traditionally a pantomime character, usually disguised and wearing a mask. Young Quin, physically powerful like the idealized men of Service's other thrillers, finds himself involved in opposition to the widespread machinations of a mysterious gangster, and is compelled to find refuge in the various hideouts of criminals in Paris. He is protected by Julot the *apache* and the bright-haired Casque d'Or. Thus Quin illustrates Service's favourite theme about fiction writing; he *lives out* his novel *Garbage,* experiencing realism and "living romance".

The plot of the book is a cinematic sequence of melodramatic incidents. It combines science with gangster fiction. The master of the microbe is an old professor who has discovered how to propagate the microbe of the Polish flu or grippe and, by spreading it, to wipe out millions of people in France and possibly in the world. He has also prepared a serum or vaccine by which to control any epidemic. The secret of propagation is in a *carnet,* and the secret of the serum is in a well-hidden silver cylinder.

Many people die in an epidemic in Paris after the professor is killed and dismembered by the gang of habitual cutthroats serving the big boss who is known only as "Sinistra." This cunning, rich, and mysterious gangster wishes to gain untold millions by selling both the *carnet* and the serum to a rather vague but dangerous power aiming at world domination.

Sinistra's murders and his raids, however, do not give him the silver cylinder required for control by those who wish to administer it. His tentacles reach out to Harley Quin, who has an apartment in the building where the deceased professor lived, and Harley also bears, unknown to himself, a certain family relationship to the mysterious Sinistra. With almost incredible ingenuity, amazing luck, and the help of Julot and Casque d'Or, Quin leads the assassins in a thrilling Hollywood chase through the underworld, and, of course, discovers the silver cylinder as well as the identity of Sinistra. Moreover, his rich cousin Rosemary, with whom he had fallen in love during an idyllic mid-May at Royat in Auvergne, is restored to him, and they are married. (It is most probable that Rosemary was idealized and separated from the sordidness of the Parisian underworld because Service associated her with Royat.) Julot, the *apache*, now going straight, wins Casque d'Or. So *The Microbe* ends with the Parisian paradise restored, as it had been in the poem entitled "Julot the Apache" in the springtime section of *Ballads of a Bohemian*.

Always in the summer there was for Service the Eden of Brittany, which had not yet received his tribute of a novel. In 1927, he gave the last of his thrillers to Finistère. It was called *The House of Fear*. He dedicated this romance

*To My Mother*
*Who in spite of her seventy odd years*
*Can still enjoy*
*A Tale of Mystery and Crime.*

The central character of this book, the Hon. Peter MacBeth, is evidently not to be identified in any way with Peter McQuattie, although both Service's rich friend and Service himself had "conky hearts." In the novel, the Hon. Peter suffers from the very pains of a cardiac condition detailed by Service about himself in *Why Not Grow Young?*, and he practices some of the same remedial routines. In other ways also,—his avuncular relationship with the heroine, his patience, his selfless daring, and his self-sacrificing disposition—he reflects Service and what Service admired in a man over fifty years of age.

The story begins, as the other novels do, in a meeting with a girl who looks interesting. The opening passage is in the Parisian area of Belleville, east of Montmartre, the setting for parts of *The Master of the Microbe*, and then shifts to Brittany, where the Hon. Peter enjoys the rugged coastal scenery not many miles west of Lancieux and Service's own restful paradise at "Dream Haven."

*The House of Fear* is anything but restful, for the large "White House" which the Hon. Peter buys on impulse, near the fishing village of Auberon and the farming village of Tremorac, is the scene for murders of the most gruesome kind. The macabre is exploited to the limit in suspicious characters, the symbolic menace of moonlight nights, faces at the window, horrible shapes bending over sleeping persons, footsteps and screams, brutal assaults, bestial smells, secret hideouts, underground passages in old "gothic" mansions, odd disappearances, strange burials, evil eyes, mesmeric demon-possession, horrible masks and werewolves, together with a further roundup of all the kinds of villainy and duplicity which Service had put into his stories of the Parisian underworld. There was also a detective. One hopes that Service's mother was satisfactorily kept awake by this work of her son!

*The House of Fear* displays a consistency of mood and purpose and an improved pace of action and speech. Most readers who prefer thrillers may still find this the most satisfactory of Service's novels; it is a book hard to lay down before the dénouement is reached. The conversation in sentimental scenes is still awkward and stiff, but most of the pages are enlivened by an uncommon amount of dialogue. There is little variety to characterize the speakers, for Service may have been somewhat inhibited by the fact that he was using English to represent French and Breton conversation.

A measure of sympathy is evoked for the ailing Peter and for Pascaline (this time, a black-haired heroine), for they must bear the savage assaults which for the armchair reader are only thrills. The fantasy of this romance finds its true anchor of credibility in Service's affectionate picturing of the Breton coast and the vivid descriptions of mysterious local eccentrics.

Peter and Pascaline are standing on the cliffs overlooking the sea, "a blade of blue steel glittering between the level of the sand and the lift of the sky," and they see "a white sail and the smoke of a steamer." Here is "space, freedom, and the salt in the breeze." They go down the uneven steps to the beach. "Above them the great root of an oak clutched the cliff like an octopus, while ivy climbed halfway down the rock. As they sat in the shadow, before them was flung the far level of sunlit sand."[11]

> There was not a cloud in all the grey-blue sky, and where the yellow-brown hillside swept up to it, two of the three windmills were turning, while the spire of Tremorac was like a silver spear-point. Huddled under the protecting hill, Auberon seemed asleep in the lazy sunshine, and its fisher-boats lay tilted on the sand. Far away, near the edge of the water, they could distinguish a cluster of black figures.

An old fisherman approaches:

> He was tall and gaunt with a sallow face and long grey beard. He stooped slightly, as if afflicted with rheumatism. This ackward gait was made more marked by pointed wooden shoes. His clothes were worn, sun-faded, sea-stiffened. From the shadow of a peaked cap his eyes regarded them with a steady stare. It was his eyes that surprised them. They were grey, a grim shark-grey, with just a hint of shark cruelty in them. Otherwise his appearance was rather venerable. Over his arm he carried a wicker basket.

Such meticulous detail concerning other persons on a social level above that of this "Ancient Mariner" caused unexpected trouble for Service.[12] The author's receipts for the novel were reduced by the threat of a suit for libel, for allegedly slandering the reputation of "a certain member of a well-known family." Rather than fight the case, Service paid the sum demanded. H. G. Wells, with whom he lunched at Grasse, disagreed, declaring that the suit should have been contested. Service's satisfaction lay in the accomplishment of this warm tribute to the natural beauty of one more of his Edens.

*The House of Fear* (1927) and its predecessor, *The Master of the Microbe,* were never filmed, but both were moneymakers. These two novels, however, marked the end of Service's career as a writer of fiction. The Metro-Goldwyn-Mayer movie of *The Trail of '98,* released in New York in March 1928, was the last of his films. And *The Collected Verse,* published by Ernest Benn in 1930 and *The Complete Poems,* published by Dodd, Mead in 1933, could have been taken as signs of the end of his verse making, and there seemed to be confirmation of this view in *Bar-Room Ballads* (1940), if it was considered a collection of leftover Yukon stories. Many people thought that Service was dead.

Paris saw little of him after he gave up the Pantheon apartment in 1929. The family's motor trips across France continued, from Lancieux to Nice, and back again. They enjoyed going through Royat and driving on the by-ways of France along many different routes. At "Dream Haven" and in Nice, Robert lived as much as possible out-of-doors and he walked more than before his illness, on his daily trysts with nature and on visits to his friends. In 1931 he took an apartment on the rue Dante in Nice.

Among his acquaintances on the Riviera was his old friend Peter McQuattie, who had married an heiress and possessed a villa in Vence. Through this transformed Bohemian, Service met Byron Binns, an old music hall star; Rex Ingram, a writer, sculptor, and actor; George Robey, who was playing Sancho Panza for a film; Laddie Cliff, another actor; Frank Harris and Robert Scully, who was "ghosting Harris' book on Bernard Shaw"; Frieda Lawrence (D. H. Lawrence was dying in a hospital) and, among others, Emma Goldman the anarchist, who had written an autobiography.

# 8 New Adventures

Service's adult life may be seen as a series of adventures alternating with periods of contemplation. As he grew older he saw no reason to anticipate an early end to this rhythmical pattern. When a publisher advised him that a summing up of his life should soon be made, he argued that he should wait for "more to say" at the age of ninety:[1] "No man should attempt autobiography before sixty, for by then his youth will be so remote he can lie about it with impunity. Better put it off till seventy, when he may begin to believe his own stories."

At the age of seventy, therefore, when he was in Hollywood, during the second World War, he tackled this form of fiction, and recorded in *Ploughman of the Moon* his memories of his Scottish and early North American experiences of the first forty years. The adventures of the next thirty-five years, spent mainly in Europe, were left for the sequel, *Harper of Heaven*. After that, during the last decade of his life, until he died in 1958, he was adventurous chiefly "in memory."

Some of the literary works of the *Harper* period have been reviewed in our chapters five to seven. Frequent references have been made to the notebooks which Service filled wherever he went, since these are the documentary sources for nearly all the information which we now possess concerning the author's life during the 1920s, 1930s, and early 1940s. The original notebooks have disappeared, but one can guess at the contents of those which were absorbed imaginatively into the novels and the poems. Also, since Service seems to have had some of his diaries with him when he wrote the two autobiographies, the chapters on the Mackenzie trip in *Ploughman* and many more chapters in *Harper* appear to have been transcribed rather directly from notebooks. In this way, he published some compositions which saw print in no other way.

More than half of *Harper of Heaven* appears to have been constructed in this fashion. There is a block of twenty-five chapters about his two visits to Communist Russia, which could be lifted out and made into a separate book. A much smaller block of four chapters deals with the experiences of Service and his family during the second World War; and a final group of five chapters records their return to the Riviera and Brittany, where he died in his eighty-fifth year.

He had gone to Russia in 1937 and 1938, when he was nearly sixty-five years of age.[2] All around him in Nice, and indeed in Europe, rightist and leftist tension was acute. He had seen mobs clashing with mobs in Nice. The papers were full of Hitler in Germany, Mussolini in Italy, and Stalin in Russia; in Spain there was civil war. Service hated ex-

tremism; he was "no political bug." Both Tories
and Reds jarred on him; he wished to be neutral
and keep his wealth. His sympathies were on the
side of the poor: he pitied the "inarticulate masses"
but "was not prepared to help them" by approving
of those who professed to lead them.

For the sake of personal safety while observing
turmoil in the streets, he left his monocle at home
and wore a beret and sweater. He decided to go to
Soviet Russia with an open mind to know the truth
for himself, whether it was an "earthly paradise" or
"an anti-chamber of hell." He found the way open
to him under the wing of Intourist, the Soviet
agency for visitors, and under that wing he saw
what he was shown, and anything else he could see
for himself.

His account is unpretentious: he tried to avoid
being a political commentator. His chapters in
*Harper* are an edited diary about the minutiae of
travelling and of observing people.[3] They reveal
Service's personality and habits as much as they reveal the Russians'. In other ways, this record is obviously dated and now of only slight historical interest, for great changes have taken place in the
Soviet Union since 1937 and 1938. Service was not
the only traveller admitted at that time, although
he was sometimes given VIP treatment alone in an
expensive car with a beautiful girl as his Intourist
guide. When there were other foreign travellers
being escorted along with him, they were usually
Communists from the United States; among the
exceptions were "Mrs. Tacoma," probably a lecturer, "Mr. Missouri," a retired storekeeper, and
"the Drummer," who exercised his charm on
blondes while Service was content to watch them.

He went to Russia in July 1937, by way of Co-
penhagen, Stockholm, and Helsinki. He had cho-

sen the official tour in and around Leningrad and Moscow. He was very well lodged at first-class hotels, and transported to interesting places under the personal care of guides, who were almost always "silk stocking socialists," well-trained, intelligent, and obliging, but incessantly propagandist about Communist superiority and capitalist crimes against humanity. Service did not engage in long arguments, but he recorded his impressions: "I like Russians but I dislike Communists." "In Russia, just as in France, the women are more capable than the men. In the peasant woman is crystallized the virtue of the race." There was still a great deal of poverty among the workers in the city and the peasants on the farms. Yet the latter seemed happier than anyone else: the doctrinaire Marxists "lacked a sense of humour."

Relics of Czarism were exhibited as object lessons concerning a detestable past. Service acknowledged that "at the thought of Czarism I become an ardent Communist;" yet, in the private rooms of the Czar and his family at Pushkin, he felt "a sincere pity" for the human beings who had lived there.

Concerning regimentation, which was making Russia a strong industrial and military power, he wrote:[4]

> *That part of me which is logical believes in a*
> *scientific organization of Society, in economic*
> *planning, in classless co-operation—all that*
> *stuff that sounds like claptrap. My mind*
> *approves of it but my heart hates it. I would*
> *loathe to be regimented and restricted. I only*
> *admire reform in other people.*

He felt in Russia, and on his way home through Berlin, that something menacing was under way: "God help us some day." Return to

France meant breathing the exhilarating air of freedom again, and happy days with his family as he joined them in late September at "Dream Haven" and made the annual trip by automobile through Tours, Royat, and Avignon to their home in Nice. There he could look forward to six months of happiness: walks in the high hills, chats with Peter McQuattie and other friends, and just enough work to make him enjoy "the careless rapture of the south."

But Russia was not easily dismissed; he found himself typing out the beginning of a novel, "FOUR BLIND MICE . . . Chapter One." "It was to be an Escape Story and to have a Russian setting." But he discovered that he knew too little of the country. Thereupon he booked for Intourist's "most elaborate" trip. "This time," he wrote, "it was to be more Oppenheimish."

On this second journey, in 1938, he travelled through Aachen, Berlin (where he had a bad time with customs men), and Poland (where a friendly mouse-like girl robbed him of his money). After crossing the Soviet border, he was on a Russian train with Louis and Myra Gutzmann, Communists from New York. In Moscow, where he spent two weeks in "atrocious" summer heat, he was taken through fifty-three pavilions and other show places of the Great Russian Exhibition. Next on the tour came Gorki (formerly Nijni-Novgorod) and a view of huge industries with scientific organization of manpower. At the beginning of a boattrip on the Volga, his party, which included the Gutzmanns, was joined by the Buntings from Brooklyn (Pop, "a regular Babbit," Ma, "a matronly Daughter of the Revolution" and Babe, their studious son—ready-made characters for a novel!)

If Service was storing up material for a thriller with a love interest, he had a demonstration going on before his very eyes as Babe and Lydia, the beautiful Intourist guide, carried on an absorbing, but hopeless, courtship. Service made serious efforts to study the Russian *bourgeoisie*, the workers, the peasants, and even the gypsies in the steerage of the Volga boat, but his diary clearly shows that he was distracted by observing the comely guides and his travelling companions. That is, when he was not devoting whole pages of his notebook to daily details about his meals, his bedrooms, and the nauseating lavatories he found everywhere except in the plush hotels. Also, preoccupied as he was with literature, he expressed his critical opinions about Myra Gutzmann's copy of *Confessions of a Nymphomaniac* by tossing the book into the Volga, while that river was flowing on undisturbed past industrial plants and small villages.

The tourists visited Kuibyshev (formerly Samara) notable in the diary chiefly for Pop Bunting's futile search for "a Service Station with a retiring room for males," and then Stalingrad (formerly Tsaritsyn, and, since 1961, Volgograd). Here the other travellers and Lydia went their own ways, and Service took a train on which he met "a new type of Russian," a stalwart farmer and his handsome son. Saratov looked listless and forlorn, but gay and pleasant Rostov, a seaport on the Don near the sea of Azov, became his "pick of Soviet cities." He was delighted with the guide assigned to him, the most glamorous woman he had seen in Russia, for whom he felt "it must have been rather a nuisance to have to waste her sweetness on [his] silver hair." All the information she gave him about Rostov, he admitted, he "could almost write on a postage stamp—though she took half a day to tell it."

Things were different as his tour took him farther into Russia: an argumentative young boy of sixteen was his guide at Orginikidzi, and the driver of a battered old car was his chauffeur over the mountains at the Georgian Pass to Tiflis. Going on by train to Batoum, he reached the shore of the Black Sea, where he went bathing. Here he was shocked on seeing nude bathers. He would have retreated, he said, had he not forced himself to look at the sight "from an *aesthetic* angle."

Material for his new romance was certainly accumulating, but the pressure for escape of a different kind, soon to become a political necessity, was approaching. On the Black Sea steamer he met a Polish prince, who was nervous about impending war. They visited Theodosia briefly, and disembarked at Yalta. There Louis Gutzmann told Service that the Germans and Russians had signed a peace pact: war was coming and Poland was doomed. Odessa was blacked out, but there was still sightseeing at Kiev. A gay company of Parisians were insensitive to coming disaster, but Service prepared to leave at once on trains to Warsaw, Berlin, and Paris.

The trip homeward turned out to be an escape indeed—realistic material, if he wanted it, for a thriller about spies crossing frontiers in times of international tension. There were many scenes of frustration, fear, and some comedy as Service and a few companions (generous "Mrs. Moosejaw" from the Canadian west and "Donald Duck," a Communist freeloader from Glasgow) came by train to the Polish border and travelled across that doomed country to the closed borders of Germany. They went on by any route by chance available to them: through Vilna to Riga (Latvia) and Tallinn (Estonia), by steamer across the Baltic to Stockholm, by train to Bergen on the Atlantic, and on a Canadian Pacific boat to Newcastle. Service took a

channel boat to Boulogne and a train to Paris and
Nice.

He and his family spent the winter of 1939-40,
as they had done since 1931, in their home in Nice,
"a beautiful house in the Place Franklin." Peter
McQuattie, their long-time friend, died during that
time and was buried near D. H. Lawrence. (Frieda
Lawrence was one of the celebrities to whom
McQuattie had introduced Service near Nice;
James Joyce, working on *Ulysses,* was another.) At
first, in southern France, war seemed far enough
away, but preparations for a new escape had to be
made.[5] The Services reached Paris, where there
were rumours of French retreats, and they found a
train for Rennes; a car took them the rest of the
way to "Dream Haven."

Refugees from northern France were beginning to flee as far as Brittany; the Belgian army
had laid down its arms. Soon the war came very
close; Rennes was bombed, and wounded British
soldiers were about to be placed on four cargo
ships at the wharf in St. Malo. Within a few hours,
Service and his family had packed some posses-
sions, locked up their house at "Dream Haven,"
and driven to St. Malo, where they carried their
bags to the wharf, and secured passage on one of
the ships, the *Hull Trader,* bound for Weymouth in
England. The Germans were then only a few miles
from Lancieux, and would soon take over the Services' Coast Guard cottage as their local headquarters. London was blacked out, and bombs were
dropping; their Chelsea flat was destroyed shortly
after Service and his family left for Liverpool en
route to Canada and to California for "the dura-
tion."

They arrived at "an eastern Canadian port"
and Robert was interviewed by the Canadian Press

on August 1st, 1940. He told the reporter that he had no desire to write about the war which had come so close to his home. Other plans had been shattered. He told his interviewer that he had recently written at Lancieux forty-thousand words of a new novel which had the French National Lottery as "the basis for the plot." The manuscript, he believed, had fallen into the hands of the Germans.

The trip across Canada was full of surprises. In Montreal he was met by his brother, Stanley, whom he had not seen for twenty years and who was now a doctor practising medicine in Ottawa. In Toronto he was welcomed and entertained as a celebrity.[6] In Vancouver he saw his sister Agnes. Many people professed to think that he was a ghost, for they casually associated his name with *Rhymes of a Red Cross Man* and assumed that the Lieutenant Service killed in action in France in 1916 was Robert. In fact the deceased brother's name was Albert. Robert's life in "glorious incognito" far away in Europe had added to the confusion.

In Canada, some of the prestige of the Sourdough poems had become attached to the "real Sam McGee," the old-time Yukoner whose name Service had drawn at random from the bank ledger when he was composing his "Cremation."[7] At one time a shack in Whitehorse had been turned into a tearoom bearing this sign: "Have a cup of tea with the ghost of Sam McGee." The real man was a copper miner and a road builder, and spent many later years in Montana. By a strange coincidence, McGee died at Beiseker in Alberta, during the first week of September, 1940, while Service was sojourning in Vancouver on his way to Hollywood. So one famous ghost had an opportunity to salute the other!

The family arrived in Hollywood late in December 1940 and found an attractive little bungalow, "two blocks from the High School." It became their home for five years, until the war in Europe had come to an end.[8] Robert's life, as private as he could make it, is described in delightful detail in *Harper of Heaven.* During the first four years, he said, he did not write a line. He indulged in his old habits of walking, watching people on the streets, and reading in the public library. The printing presses, however, had not been idle, for Ernest Benn in London and Dodd, Mead in New York brought out his *Bar-Room Ballads* in 1940, and the American firm also published his "Complete Poems" in 1942.

His daughter ran the house with great efficiency; Mrs. Service went to classes at the high school and worked for the Red Cross; Robert, faced with the necessity of making some American dollars, did some work as a lecturer, reciter, and radio broadcaster, for which he studied voice control with a retired Shakespearean actor. It was in 1942 that he had his own moment as an actor on the screen in *The Spoilers,* a play by Lawrence Hazard and Tom Reed, adapted from the novel by Rex Beach.

It was directed by Ray Enright and produced by Frank Lloyd for Universal Pictures. A review in *The New York Times* described it as "a lovely brawl"—an "extravaganza of tough men and headstrong women in the Klondike gold rush ... fought along distinctly primeval lines of etiquette."[9]

The tough men were played by Randolph Scott and John Wayne. Glamour was adequately supplied by Marlene Dietrich. Service was enlisted as "The Poet," engaged in writing his ballad of Dan

McGrew. He was to have twenty-three words of conversation with Cherry Malotte (the divine Marlene), who was to ask him whether he was writing about her. His reply was to be "No, not about you *this* time, Cherry." After much coaching, much worry and little success in controlling his voice, he dressed himself in a costume that was "a cross between a miner, a cowboy, a rough-rider, and Billy the Kid," and, behind a Hollywood make-up, he faced the golden Dietrich on the set. The director's opinion of his effort was brief and to the point: "It's lousy, but we'll let it go." It was the "Big Fight" that made the picture famous.[10]

Service's postscript to *Ploughman of the Moon* indicates that he began writing this autobiography on Halloween in 1943 and that he completed it on Halloween in 1944. It was started "as an experiment in Escape" from Hollywood literary activities and from worries about the war: remembering the past helped him to forget the present. So much was recalled in this "adventure into memory" (the subtitle) that he made a record covering only his first forty years, up to the time when he left Dawson forever. This book, *Ploughman of the Moon*, was published in 1946 with a dedication "to the Memory of My Father",

> Full of rich earthiness, a Grand Old Guy,
> With all his faults a better man than I.

The title came from a poem by Verlaine:

> Pedlar of dream-stuff, piping an empty tune;
> Fisher of shadows, Ploughman of the Moon.

When France was free again, Robert applied for visas to take himself and his family home to France; this official process took four months, through most of the winter of 1946. An article in the *Toronto Star* of September 11, 1958, states that

Robert visited three of his brothers in Canada at this time (1946). One may suppose that he saw Alexander (a retired electrical engineer) and Peter (a second-hand bookshop proprietor) in Vancouver, for they were residents of that city where their mother had spent her last days. Perhaps Ottawa was also on Robert's route from Chicago to New York, for the *Star* mentions a visit with Stanley, the brother who was a doctor in Ottawa.

An Atlantic crossing was not easy to arrange, but an opportunity to go aboard a troop ship came suddenly, giving them only two days to complete their shopping and other arrangements in New York. As unofficial passengers on a naval vessel, they had a rather uncomfortable voyage across the Atlantic, although they were hospitably cared for by the officers. One of the entertainments on board was the film of *The Spoilers*; in mid-ocean Service saw himself in conversation with Marlene and was roundly applauded for his effort.

He was seriously ill when they landed in Marseilles just before Christmas. As they waited in discomfort and impatience for a train, they worried about the fate of their apartment in Nice. Upon their arrival, they found their home and treasures miraculously unharmed. Even the manuscripts of three unpublished books were safe in a strong box in a local bank. There was a great scarcity of food and other commodities in that cold post-war winter on the Riviera, but they were sustained by parcels from the Red Cross and from friends in the United States and Canada. Spring brought the old "radiant living" once more.

"Dream Haven" had not fared so well, for, on the return of the Services to Brittany for the summer of 1947, they found that their Lancia was safe in a garage, but their house had been looted by the

Germans very soon after the family's escape in
1940:

> *the best of my Savile Row suits . . . Our silver
> and napery, our linen, embroidery, pictures,
> our carpets, curtains, clothes and shoes—all
> disappeared in a twinkling . . . my
> accordion. . . . My grand piano, a Steinway,
> was shipped to Hamburg; my guitars, my
> motor bicycle were grabbed with delight.*

Twenty-five soldiers had occupied their "Coast
Guard" house:

> *. . . when Rommel came on a tour of
> inspection it was made a defensive point . . . to
> be converted into a citadel . . . a fortress.*

At the end of the occupation, the Germans,
driven out by the Americans, had not had time to
blow up the house, but it was a wreck, not quite a
skeleton. It was restored, and remained Service's
summer home until he died there on September
11th, 1958. His ambition to live a hundred years
was not fulfilled; his heart failed when he was
eighty-four. His beloved Haven was not deserted
after he had to leave it; the rue Robert Service in
Lancieux leads up to the old house on the point
where Mrs. Service preserves her memories of
their happy marriage, and to a neighbouring
house, where the members of her family still spend
their summers.

In 1946, Service changed his Riviera home
from Nice to Monte Carlo, and it is there that his
daughter Iris, her husband Mr. J. L. Davies, and
their daughters Anne and Armelle, now have their
own winter home, not many streets away from Mrs.
Service's "Villa Aurora." The name of that house
appears on a letter which the poet wrote on May
20th, 1951, to Professor Thomas Greenwood of

*Germaine Service*

Villa Aurora, the Services' home in Monte Carlo.

the University of Montreal in reply to a request for biographical information.[11]

Service advised the professor to use *Who's Who*. This is how he described his last years: "I have, however, published two books, running to 800 pages which contain all I want to be known of my life story. . . . I fear I am not much interested in myself personally, and getting to an age when I am too tired to do any other work but the poem I write every few days."

He also knew how much of himself he had revealed obliquely to perceptive readers as his books had circulated in millions of copies during his lifetime. Some of these works still circulate in thousands of copies in 1975.

The end of his production in prose came in 1948 with the publication of *Harper of Heaven* by Dodd, Mead of New York. It was his hail and farewell to Europe: a collection of chapters drawn sometimes directly from his notebooks and diaries, enriched by his mature good humour, his wisdom, and his emphasis on "radiant living."

For such "radiant living" and for the fervent composition of prose or verse which it inspired, he had a symbol growing out of his life-long love of music:

> *With eyes of ecstasy I see*
> *And hear the Harps of Heaven.*

He knew that he had been fortunate beyond the dreams of most other men. Over the long story of his life, he saw his destiny collaborating with him, and himself collaborating with his destiny. An optimistic outlook was possible to the very "End of the Trail." In his fifties, his cardiac trouble had prompted him to make a public statement of his private philosophy in *Why Not Grow Young?*:

*Germaine Service*

Robert Service with his concertina, Monte Carlo, 1956.

"So in my seventies this is what life means to me," he wrote, as he prepared to conclude *Harper of Heaven* (1948) with a passage drawn, almost word for word, from the 1928 volume:

*Happiness, in whatever form it comes, is not to be questioned. It is to be hugged to the heart. Illusion is to be cherished. On the surface of things is enchantment enough. . . .*

*Surely a faith in our Universe and our human destiny should satisfy us. Let us then put all futile gropings for a meaning of life out of our minds and come down to the pure joy of living. Let us worship Nature as she reveals herself in all simplicity and beauty. And if we live in usefulness and sanity according to her laws, cultivating happiness and sharing it with those near and dear to us, we will do more than well. The measure of our sunshine is the brightness we can kindle in the eyes of others.*

*In some cloistered garden we may walk with peace, and in the joy of little things our vain efforts to comprehend the Universe may be forgotten. In tangible beauty is charm and solace. In visible nature is comfort. Let us be eager to be pleased; grateful for every gleam of sunshine. Nature can comfort us and bring us joy. Are we not her children? Let us try, if it so pleases us, to understand her with the minds of sages, but let us enjoy her with the hearts of children.*

*So in the end let us seek a quiet home, and with earth radiant about us, face the setting sun. With thankful eyes and grateful hearts let us rejoice that it has been granted to us to live the length of our years in a world of beauty—to understand much, to divine much, and to come at last through pleasant paths to peace. Peace and understanding! So with our last gaze let us face the serene sunset, content to have played our parts and saying humbly:*

*"Nature from whose bosom I come, take me back tenderly, lovingly, Forgive my faults, my failures, and now that my usefulness to you is ended, grant me to rest eternally."*

*ALL IS WELL*

# 9 Songs in Autumn

Two poems, *Dan McGrew* and *Sam McGee*, had brought Robert Service fame and fortune. They had given him the freedom to pursue a career of rhyming which lasted fifty years and yielded more than two thousand pages of printed verse. Late in his life he estimated wryly that he had written thirty thousand couplets, and employed more than ten thousand rhymes. Three very large volumes are still being sold, bearing the titles *Collected Poems*, *More Collected Verse*, and *Later Collected Verse*. The first of these contains his production up to 1940; the second one, from 1945 to 1953; the third, from 1953 to 1958. At least seven hundred poems were originally published after 1949, when he was between seventy-five and eighty-four years of age.

The *Collected Verse* (1930) and *The Complete Poems* (1933) were succeeded by *Collected Poems*, copyrighted by the author in 1940. *The Bar-Room Ballads* (1940) were made Book Six in this new collection, but the inconsequential *Twenty Bath-Tub*

171

*Ballads* (1939) were omitted. These facts indicate a hiatus in his writing of verse, certainly in his publication of verse, between *Ballads of a Bohemian* (1921) and 1940—that is, through the "thriller" twenties, the possibly lazy thirties, and the war-time forties. It is difficult, however, to determine how many verses written during the hiatus went into the first volumes of Service's post-war series of poetic books which began with *Songs of a Sun-Lover,* published in 1949. Not much, therefore, can be said to identify any poetic production of the Nice and second Hollywood periods, which ended in 1946. In that year, with the removal of Service's household to Monte Carlo,[1] the remarkable Monaco period began.

This Monaco verse has considerable biographical and critical value, for it rounds out, on Service's own terms, the story of his life and thought. Most of it was published in separate volumes before the large collected editions were made. In the various titles, the sacred word "poem" is conspicuously avoided: *Songs of a Sun-Lover* (1949); *Rhymes of a Roughneck* (1950), *Lyrics of a Lowbrow* (1951), *Rhymes of a Rebel* (1952), *Songs For My Supper* (1953), *Carols of an Old Codger* (1954), *Rhymes For My Rags* (1956), and *Cosmic Carols* (1957?).

The first five of these volumes (publications of the years 1949 to 1953) were bound together in *More Collected Verse* in 1955.[2] The remaining ones *(Carols of an Old Codger, Rhymes For My Rags,* and *Cosmic Carols)* were reprinted posthumously, accompanied by "Verse From Prose Writings" and "Selections From Unpublished Verse," in *Later Collected Verse* of 1960. The division at the year 1955 may have been largely a matter of convenience, or it may have been an indication that the aged minstrel had not yet given up the habit of composing

*Dodd, Mead & Company*

Robert Service sent this picture of himself to his New York publisher with the following note on the back:

> *Alas! My belly is concave,*
> *My locks no longer wavy;*
> *But though I've one foot in the grave*
> *The other's in the gravy.*

> Robert Service,
> crowding eighty-four.

My birthday Jan 16-1958 might inspire some modest publicity for me on your part.

several songs or ballads every week. He evidently accomplished this remarkable feat with no sense of strain. He amused himself by rhyming and singing lines to himself with the accompaniment of a guitar or ukelele or piano accordion "for an imaginary audience"—often in the dark.

All of these later publications show that Service was surveying his past in terms of the present in which he found himself. *Songs of a Sun-Lover* (1949) seems to be related in a special way to the prose works of the 1940s, when he was turning his attention from Paris to the south of France, and, with the fresh experiences of war-time residence in North America, writing his biographies, *Ploughman of the Moon* (1946) and *Harper of Heaven* (1948). Some of the songs in *A Sun-Lover* may have been "harped" in the early 1940s. Certainly this book is dedicated to Provence: "O Land of Song! O golden clime!" In a lyric for his seventy-fifth birthday on the 16th of January, 1949, he was in a mood to "whoop it up" and let the world know that he was still alive. Coming to terms with his destiny was going to be necessary, but chiefly as part of an ongoing career in song.

*Songs of a Sun-Lover* gave him an opportunity to reappear as the same old poet with an even stronger assertion of his aims. His *apologia* for his early and his forthcoming verse runs through this first of the Monaco books; it is most clearly stated in "A Verseman's Apology",

> *Alas! I am only a rhymer,*
> *I don't know the meaning of Art;*
> *But I learned in my little school primer*
> *To love Eugene Field and Bret Harte.*
> *I hailed Hoosier Ryley with pleasure,*
> *To John Hay I took off my hat;*

*These fellows were right to my measure,*
*And I've never gone higher than that.*

. . . . . . . . . . . . . . . . . . . . . . . . . . . . . .

*For God-sake don't call me a poet,*
*For I've never been guilty of that.*

. . . . . . . . . . . . . . . . . . . . . . . . . . . . . .

*And I fancy my grave-digger griping*
*As he gives my last lodging a pat:*
*"That guy wrote McGrew;*
*'Twas the best he could do"* . . .
*So I'll go to my Maker with that.*

In an intermediate stanza he declared that

*The Classics! Well, most of them bore me*
*The Moderns I don't understand;*
$\qquad\qquad\qquad\qquad$ *(MCV, SL56)*

There was some over-statement in this; he
knew, for example, what a Pullman porter at Montreal meant when that polished servant of travellers
declared that he owned all of Service's books of
verse, but his taste was "Eliot and Auden". In
"Book-Lover" Service gave an impressive list of
great authors on his library shelves which he now
no longer read. In "My Library" he confessed with
shame that he was too old to read his thousand
books, but that he "wallowed" in "the Daily Press."
It was part of his programme for living and writing
in the world of the present day with plenty of time
for communion with nature. In this way he hoped
to stay in touch with "simple folk" and in his "va-
grant singing"

*I take the clay of every day*
*And mould it in my fashion;*
*I seek to trace the commonplace*
*With humour and compassion.*
*Of earth am I, and meekly try*
*To be supremely human:*

*To please, I plan, the little man,*
*And win the little woman.*

*(MCV, SL 2)*

A few Yukon ballads, included in *Sun-Lover*, showed that this was indeed the McGrew and McGee storyteller that readers remembered. The comedy was in Service's coarsest vein, and he added to his Northern characterizations the first of a series of effective ballads about Montreal Maree, a dance hall girl "as pretty as a pansy, wi' a heart o' Hunker gold." The tuneful lyric about "Marie Vaux of the Painted Lips" is a welcome addition to this book: under the title of "The Last Supper" it had first appeared in *The Trail of Ninety-Eight* as the work of the "Pote", Ollie Gaboodler. Service was now claiming it as his own. There is further sympathy for fallen women in "Babette", "No Lilies for Lisette", and "White Christmas"; these evidently belong to the Bohemian period. There are also compassionate portrayals of the various unhappy fates of an actor, a millionaire, a little Jewish orphan, an opera singer, a tippler, a murderer, a motorcycle racer and his girl, a boxer, and the deserted sweetheart of a soldier boy. Service's portrait gallery, already packed with distinctively drawn likenesses of a host of characters, would have many more additions before he laid down his pen.

In *Sun-Lover* Service displayed a growing tendency to make explicit attacks upon war, political injustices, and oppression of the poor. The realism with which he now went to the heart of a matter was sharper than the realism of setting in the thrillers, or the realism of human activity in the earlier vignettes. But his ideas were still incorporated in the doings of men and women, often through the device of using these characters as the ostensible speakers of the lines of a poem. His favourite technique involved a brief, effective presentation of a situation followed by an expression of the consequences thereof in a rhetorical or ironic ending. He was tireless in his search for the unique word or phrase.

"Tranquility" is one of many examples of irony. In the first three lines everything is serene: the speaker walks beside the sea, where a fisherman, a mother and child, and a grey-haired painter are enjoying themselves:

> *Yet in my Morning Rag I read*
> *Of paniked peoples, dark with dread,*
> *Of flame and famine near and far,*
> *Of revolution, pest and war;*
> *The fall of this, the rise of that,*
> *The writhing proletariat . . .*
> . . . . . . . . . . . . . . . . . . . . . . . . . .
> *Alas, what mockery for me!*
> *Can peace be mine till Man be free?*
> *(MCV, SL 52-3)*

For an example of vivid imagery, one may turn to "Worms", concerned with the pitiful condition of the poor in the city slums.

By way of contrast, he repeatedly described, and sometimes sardonically worried about, his own happy situation in the south:

> *Here in this vale of sweet abiding,*
> *My ultimate and dulcet home,*

his garden, the birds, his dogs, "an olive fire", delicious food and drink, and especially his home. The philosophy of the end of *Harper of Heaven* is reiterated in the rhyme of "Pantheist":

> *Yes, I am one with all I see,*
> *With wind and wave, with pine and palm;*
> *Their very elements in me*

*Are fused to make me what I am.*
*Through me their common life-stream flows,*
*And when I yield this human breath,*
*In leaf and blossom, bud and rose,*
*Live on I will . . . There is no Death.*
                                    *(MCV, SL 54)*

Many nature poets have said less in more words.

In "God's Battle-Ground" he laid the foundations of his opinions about divinity. Man is the "battle-ground":

*God lives in me, in all I feel*
*Of love and hate, of joy and pain,*
*Of grace and greed, of woe and weal,*
*Of fear and cheer, of loss and gain:*
*For good or evil I am He,*
*Yea, saint or devil, One are we.*

*God fends and fights in each of us;*
*His altars we, or bright or dim;*
*So with no sacerdotal fuss*
*But worthy act let's worship Him:*
*Goodness is Godness—let us be*
*Deserving of Divinity.*
                                  *(MCV, SL 176)*

In this way Service supported his assertion that "God did not make you . . . *You make God.*"

God is not diminished by offering to man the freedom to act in gentle kindliness or in evil ways. God being "What is," the struggle is also God's: the struggle is human and divine. Thus, for Service, life was God's experiment, and it called for active realism, not for "abstract terms," which appeared to set God at a distance from daily life. In "Agnostic Apology" he described himself as a "stout materialist":

*And so I've made a little list*
*Of words that don't make sense to me.*
*To fool my reason I refuse,*

*For honest thinking is my goal;*
*And that is why I rarely use*
*Vague words like* Soul.

*(MCV, SL 143)*

Also on his list were "Spirit" and "Creator", but he
did not dare to flout what "the stars spell out:
GOD."

There is a sense in which, for him, life and all
his writings were religious, for he was dedicated to
finding and reporting little dramas of human experience; vignettes were revelations of mingled
success and failure on an individual scale. A report
of life as lived was a form of identification with the
universe; and

*God is not outside and apart*
*From Nature, but her very heart;*
*No Architect (as I of verse)*
*He is Himself the Universe.*

*(MCV, SL 145)*

The poet is a "maker": it is his business to construct
an accurate verbal transcription of what he can see
and know. It is his mood that counts. "Goodness is
Godness," and Goodness is kindliness, compassion,
love, peace, tolerance, and opposition to tyranny
and oppression. "To fight that Mankind may be
free . . . ," he said, "There is our Immortality." It
seemed a high calling from which a versifier of the
"common" lot was not excluded.

It will not be possible to trace restatements of
these themes through all the Monaco books, although the next one, *Rhymes of a Roughneck* (1950),
shows an interesting development beyond the con-
clusion of "Prayer." Praying was not in Service's
line,

*Unless that sittin' still*
*Can be a kind o' prayer;*

*(MCV, SL 146-7)*

Yet "when the *Cross* I see/I make the sign." Some of
the later books have sections entitled "Rhymes for
Reverence." Perhaps one should not be startled
when one turns to the last page of *Roughneck* where
a ✝ appears under the title "Rhyme For My
Tomb".

> *Here lyeth One*
> *Who loved the Sun;*
> *Who lived with zest,*
> *Whose work was done.*
> *Reward, dear Lord,*
> *Thy weary son:*
> *May he be blest*
> *With peace and rest,*
> *Nor wake again,*
> *Amen.*
>
> *(MCV, RR 206)*

The *Roughneck* book may be regarded as a sup-
plement to *Sun-Lover*, for the Rhymes are grouped
under headings appropriate to both books: "Lowbrow Lyrics," "Garden Glees," "Library Lays,"
"Poems of Compassion," "Ribald Rhymes," "Vignettes in Verse," and "Mortuary Muse." A fair
choice from the numerous offerings in each of the
categories respectively would include "McCluskey's
Nell" (a Montreal Maree ballad); "My Pal" ("Brave
bird, be lyric to the last. . . . And so will I,/And so
will I"); "Amateur poet" ("To make my rhyme
come right,/And find at last the phrase
unique/Flash fulgent in my sight"); "The Under-
Dogs" ("What have we done, Oh Lord, that we/Are
evil starred?"); "Include Me Out" ("I grabbed the
new *Who's Who* to see/My name—but it was not
. . ./The book I held was *Who WAS Who*/Oh was I
glad—and how!"); "Humility" ("Yet if in sheer hu-
mility/I yield this yokel place,/Will he not think it

mockery/And spit into my face"); and "The Hand" ("How merciful a Mind/My life has planned!").

In such verses there are few significant differences from those in *Songs of a Sun-Lover*. Yet one may sense Service's growing tendency to stress the lamentable in human existence and to moralize about it; at the same time there is no retreat from the policy of illustrating nearly everything by means of vignettes and suggestive images. The pronoun "I" (so often used) belongs to his *persona*, his fictional participant, but the author's heart is in that "I" more sympathetically than ever before. He cannot resist being part of all that he had met. Also, he gives evidence of renewed and stronger literary interests: he had been recalling and rereading his favourite authors. In "God's Skallywags" he asserts that he would set Villon, Baudelaire, Byron, Poe, Wilde, Francis Thompson, and Burns high above the "merely holy" writers. He praises Maeterlinck as "a forgotten master," communes with the spirit of Thomas Hardy as one of the "Great Rejected Poets," and gives "his vote" to Cervantes rather than to Shakespeare.

One of the novel features of *Rhymes of a Roughneck* is the appearance of travel verses. The first instalment of a series which would range through several books from ribaldry to indignation was saucily entitled "Dago Ditties." As a "Tourist" he preferred "to Mike Angelo/The slim stems of a lady tourist"; and as a "Florentine Pilgrim" he thought "better than a dozen Dantes" was "something cute in female scanties." What he wrote about "The Pigeons of St. Marks" can be left to the imagination. Yet there was reverence for genius and art. The Leaning Tower of Pisa reminded him that Galileo had stood there; and the Apollo Belvedere was "A bit o'frozen music."

The third Monaco book, *Lyrics of a Lowbrow* (1951), opens with "Dawson Ditties"—exotic enough to be travel literature for Europeans—offering, among other reminiscences, a wistful catalogue of the dance hall girls who flourished long ago in the Yukon: Touch the Button Nell, Minnie Dale, Rosa Lee, Lorna Doone, Daisy Bell, Montreal Maree, Gertie of the Diamond Tooth, the Mare of Oregon, Violet de Vere, Claw-fingered Kate, and Gumboot Sue. And in "Two Men" he paid his tribute to a pair of strong northland authors, Jack London and Rex Beach.

Among Service's later travels there had evidently been a trip to Spain. Under the heading of "Spanish Serenade" he stressed his impressions of the attitude of the Spanish people to the dictatorship of General Franco. He said that the peasants had turned from politics to toil, unwilling to "pay again blood-price for Liberty"; white-collar Spaniards refrained from civil strife for their children's sake. In "Barcelona" there was a form of peace, enforced by guns. Yet "Peace can mean more than liberty . . ./Benevolent dictatorship/May be the answer, after all." But he was uneasy when he interpreted the image of a "Cat with wings," displayed by a showman in Madrid: the wings were merely rabbit ears.

> *The hell of hells is to have wings*
> *Yet be denied the bliss of flight.*
>
> *(MCV, LLB 41-2)*

The Bulls of the Corpus Christi fete represented to him the sordid passions of mankind.

The sections of *Lyrics of a Lowbrow,* however, which were given to "Rhymes for Ribaldry," "Rural Rhymes," "Vignettes in Verse," "Rhymes for Ripeness," "Rhymes for Rue," and "Rhymes For Reverence" reveal Service's sustained interest in the non-political observation of life and nature made familiar to readers of his earlier books. He had also become even more eager to explain himself. For a poet of his persuasion, "lowbrow" was a sardonic step lower than "roughneck." The "Prelude" to this third Monaco volume is more of a confession than a manifesto:

> *to lure the crowd*
> *With cap and bells I sing;*
> . . . . . . . . . . . . . . . . . . . . . . . . . . . . .
> *The lofty line will ne'er be mine*
> *To rude rhyme I belong,*
>
> . . . . . . . . . . . . . . . . . . . . . . . . . . . . .
> *A clown I go:* Houp La! *But Oh*
> *The hunger in my heart!*
>
> *(MCV, LLB 1)*

On the whole, *Lowbrow* is a typical and attractive book by the aged Robert Service, as it shows him quite happy in his Monaco and Breton retreats, still alert to what was going on around him, and still indulging in quips such as these:

> *[Rare Robbie Burns] The sinner best*
> *beloved of God—*
> *[Robert Service in "The Seance," when a*
> *fat dame remarks,]*
> *"I didn't know that he was dead."*
> *"No more did I," I sourly said.*

In "L'Envoi" to *Lowbrow* he prayed

> *O God! please let me write*
> *Just one book more.*

So the Monaco series continued. In 1952, *Rhymes of a Rebel*, the fourth book, proved that he had not signed off forever. Indeed, he returned in verse to travel and politics—sightseeing in Spain and politics in France. The group of "Songs From Seville" contains chiefly comments on tourist attractions: the tombs of the monarchs at the Escorial, the tomb of Columbus in the Cathedral, the pictures by Goya in the Prado at Madrid, a memorial for Don Juan, and bullfights on Ascension Day.

As one reads the rhymes which begin with "A Frenchman Speaks," it is well to remember that the author was an expatriate Briton (for Service had served in France under non-French flags) and that he never gave up his British citizenship. The "Frenchman" says that his father died in the first World War, that he reluctantly had to fight in the second war, and that his son might die in the third:

> *No longer patriots are we;*
> *The days of sacrifice are sped;*
> *Slaughter is worse than slavery:*
> *How cheap a hero—dead!*
>
> *(MCV, Reb 3)*

In this light, Service presents the views of a "Normandy Peasant," whose land is expropriated for military purposes; a "Volunteer" lured into the forces; a "European conscript" trapped into sacrificing himself abroad for imperial greed; and a Padre, who remembers a lad dying on the battle field—"bone is brittle, blood is red/A flag's a rag when all is said." From these anti-war poems Service moved into the field of labour. A leader in that movement says, "I'll never vote again and play the silly fool." There is compassion and resentment in such lines as

> *God help the guys as good as I*
> *Who never—get a—break.*"

and

> *Of earth-folk downward driven;*
> *Of ruthless martyrdom of man,*
> *Since human life began.*
>
> > *(MCV, Reb 25,26)*

In "Nineteen Ninety-Nine" he saw

> *a Century that dies in pain*
> *From languishing of anarchy's red reign.*
> . . . . . . . . . . . . . . . . . . . . . . . . . . . . .
> *The path of progress leads to the abyss.*
>
> > *(MCV, Reb 31-2)*

In the group of poems entitled "Lyrics of the Lost," the rebellious and compassionate mood is carried into vignettes of persons hopelessly frustrated. The losers include a battered boxer, three blind musicians, an aged fiddler, a ditch-digger, a caged lark and caged girl, an old waiter, an impoverished prince who picks up cigarette butts, an insurance "tout," a disillusioned teacher, a gardener who rejoices in a cast-off coat, and three mothers who lose their sons. The "Poems of People" are also about "what might have been."

In "Songs of Myself" and "Sylvan Songs," Service pictures himself as an "old codger" living a Rolls Royce life. He wishes that he could write real poetry (but not odes like Ezra Pound's). A poem, he says, should be like a crystal brook, a bird, a flower, but these are in themselves perfect poems. He delights in these and has "no need to write." Yet he wants five more years to taper off as a versifier. In another selection, he thanks God that he is just a man of rhyme and does not

> *seek to join the poor per cent*
> *Of goofy guys who homage pay*
> *To piddling poets of today.*
>
> > *(MCV, Reb 181)*

He plans to continue as a "rhyme-monger":

*Most everyday like egg I lay*
*A lyric smooth,*
*Of even time and ready rhyme,*
*My skill to prove.*

*(MCV, Reb 182)*

Under the heading of "Whimsicalities," he proves that he has not lost his broad sense of humour: two more ballads about Montreal Maree deserve a place beside *"McGee"* and *"McGrew."* (MCV, Reb 161 and 163)

*Songs For My Supper* (1953) was the fifth of the Monaco books and stood at the end of the collection entitled *More Collected Verse*, published in 1955 while Service was still alive and writing. The travel series was concluded here as "Soviet Strains," a group of verses supplementing the prose account of his trips to Russia in 1937 and 1938. A pleasant little ballad is made of the hopeless love affair of Wilbur, the American boy, and Olga of the Volga. The boy returns to his father's glue factory in the United States. "At Lenin's Tomb," Service repeats the warning that the great red flag is a

*Bright symbol of that crimson flood*
*One day to drench this world with blood.*

*(MCV, SS 45)*

There are several other unusual features in this book of *Songs*. Service here drops his Rolls Royce contentment and puts on the mask of a bard, eighty years of age, who must work for his bread because no one will buy his books. In fact he was very rich, but this device served to identify himself with the poor, the unemployed, the underprivileged, the prisoners of toil, the unwilling soldiers, and the doomed felons. He had experienced in early life all but the last two of these misfortunes.

The theme is, once more, resentment on behalf of those whom systems of various kinds have caged. Service was an exponent of liberty, not of equality, not of fraternity, and not of communism. He was an individualist to the end.

In "Domestic Ditties" he accepts his place as Grandpa, more or less shelved by his family, while he relives in memory some childhood scenes. "Rhymes for Irony" is his general term for paradoxes and surprise endings concerned with miscellaneous subjects ranging here from the sex obsessions of cats and the slovenliness of Beethoven to his own anger at the *Morning Star* for printing a fleshy picture of himself as a "tycoon." In "Lyrics of the Lost" and "Lyrics for Reverence," he took up the themes and methods in which he excelled, and demonstrated ever-fresh descriptions of characters and their human problems. He scrupulously avoided repetition of settings and statements.

Very much the same applies to *Carols of an Old Codger* (1954), *Rhymes For My Rags* (1956), and the undated *Cosmic Carols,* published when he was over eighty years of age and republished in *Later Collected Verse* after his death.[3] In these books he maintains the pose of a poor old man whose books are not selling because his rhymes and rhythms are outmoded. There is still a substantial number of vignettes, notably two saucy Yukon ballads: Violet de Vere, "strip-teaser of renown" is haled before a judge for raising Cain and beating up the police. Judge McGraw imposes a twenty dollar fine, which she counters in these words:

> *Judge, darlin', you've been owin' me five*
> *bucks for near a year:*
> *Take fifteen,—there! We'll call it square,"*
> *said Violet de Vere.*
>
> (*LCV, Codg 44-5*)

*Germaine Service*

Robert and Germaine Service on the balcony of the Villa
Aurora in Monte Carlo.

*Germaine Service*

One of the last pictures taken of Robert Service shows
him with (left to right) his daughter Iris, Germaine Service, and granddaughters, Anne and Armelle.

In "The Twins of Lucky Strike," Lipstick Lou died in giving birth to twins. The news creates a Christmas atmosphere in the saloon. Black Moran from Nome asserts that he will be Grandpa to the orphans. "I sink zey creep into my heart," said Montreal Maree, who holds the babes while sixty sourdoughs donate "solid pokes o' virgin gold" to hang on the babes' Christmas tree in the saloon. The ballad ends with an intriguing view of Montreal Maree "awheelin' of a double pram." (LCV, Codg 50-3)

The circle of Service's interests was also drawing more closely around his own way of living as a domesticated old man and a happy grandfather. The *Old Codger* opens with "Rhymes for Ripeness," and *Rhymes For My Rags* begins with "Songs of A Grand-Sire." The presence of a little girl in his family dispelled the gloom which, under other circumstances, might have darkened his later songs. He used the names of Lindy Lou, Annabelle, Anne, and Susie for the children of his fancy, but the first grandchild presented to him by his daughter Iris and her husband James Llewellyn Davies (formerly a Lieutenant in the R.A.F.) was named Anne, and the second baby was named Armelle. One of the most pleasing later poems, entitled "Guignol," describes Service and his "toddlers" at the Punch and Judy show.

As evidence of continuing good humour, he was still indulging in "Lyrics for Levity" and "Derisive Ditties," which were exercises in irony spreading over into "Rhymes for Resignation" about Clemenceau, Mistinguette, Ernie Pyle, Einstein, Tom Paine, Dylan [Thomas], Monticelli, and Benjamin Franklin.

Inevitably, however, he felt impelled to write postscripts on life and rhyme. He had often described his attitude toward religion as agnosticism, or simply "reverence," in the absence of certainty. As an Old Codger, he hoped

> *Aye, though a godless way I go,*
> *And sceptic is my trend,*
> *A faith in* something I don't know
> *Might save me in the end.*
>
> *(LCV, Codg 137)*

His old confidence in fate—without naming God— had weakened, and, in spite of "life's mechanistic groove," he now resolved to "play"

> *At Free Will, though we be*
> *The gnatlike creatures of a day,*
> *The dupes of Destiny . . .*
> *The merle is merry in the may—*
> *Tomorrow's time to pray.*
>
> *(LCV, Codg 153)*

In "Pragmatic," he no longer doubted the beneficence of church-going:

> *Religion may be false or true.*
> *But by the Lord—it works.*
>
> *(LCV, Codg 146)*

The "riddle of Reality," which was basic to his thinking about life and religion, had also been the key to his literary practice when he wrote vignettes, which were characterized by the dramatic interplay of favourable and unfavourable forces in human lives. He was not inclined to label much that he described as wholly good or wholly evil. The riddle of life and of lives demanded ironic treatment. This attitude is confirmed in a stanza introducing the valuable "unpublished" selections in *Later Collected Verse:*

> *I don't believe in all I write,*
> *But seek to give a point of view;*

*Am I unreasonable? Quite!*
*I'm ready to agree with you . . .*
*Times, though opponents we deride,*
*Let's try to see the other side.*
                    *(LCV, "unpublished", 415)*

He hoped that he had occasionally written a poem:

*For every verseman by mistake*
*A bit of poetry may make.*
          *(LCV, "unpublished" 433)*

Pretentious poets of his day, he believed, were actually "versemen ninety-five per cent." Then what indeed was poetry, which would have satisfied the hunger in his heart?

*Originality of phrase,*
*Imaginatively ablaze;*
*The word unique, the magic fire,*
*That haunt, illumine and inspire;*
*Not lyric lilt, nor rhyme precision,*
*Not thought, not melody,—just VISION.*
          *(LCV, "unpublished" 433)*

He'd go to his Maker with some of that!

Robert W. Service died of a heart attack in Lancieux, Brittany, on the 11th of September 1958. His body lies in a grave near "Dream Haven," the home to which long before he had given his heart.

NOTES

*Chapter 1* Ayrshire and Glasgow
1. Service's account of his boyhood and youth is in *Ploughman of the Moon* (an autobiography, 1946) pp. 1-121. References to Athol Meldrum are drawn from the novel *The Trail of Ninety-Eight* (1910) pp. v-vii and 1-51.
2. Mr. R. D. Macgregor's letter, 16 December, 1975, quoting information from the Public Relations Committee of the Preston District Council.
3. Mrs. Service's letter, 4 Dec., 1963.
4. Letter, 28 August, 1973. Ker. p. 358. Also John Hay, *Kilwinning Parish. A Short History* (1967).
5. See *Ploughman,* pp. 37-8. Many years later R. W. Service erected a tall monument of granite near the wall of the ancient abbey. It bears the names of Robert's grandfather, John Service (d. 7 May 1887, aged 75) and his grandmother, Agnes Niven (d. 3 Oct. 1883, aged 70). Five members of their family are named (their dates are only partly decipherable): Alexander (who d. 21 August, 1874); Agnes (d. 14 Nov., 1870, aged 37); Isabella, Jeanie, and Janet.
6. Information supplied by Mr. A. B. M. Scott of Glasgow.
7. Mrs. Service's letter, 15 July, 1975.
8. Letter and booklet sent 26 July, 1973 by Miss Mary B. Rodger, Secretary of Hillhead High School, Oakfield Avenue, Glasgow.
9. Letters from Mr. A. B. M. Scott of the Glasgow Chief Office of the Bank of Scotland, 17 Oct. and 5 Nov., 1974.
10. Service's *Why Not Grow Young?,* pp. 22-3.
11. See Chapter 5.
12. Letter from Mr. A. B. M. Scott, 17 Oct., 1974.

*Chapter 2.* The Nemesis of Toil
1. This important date was given by Mr. A. B. M. Scott. Additional information was supplied by Mr. Robert G. Jeffrey, Features Editor of *The Evening Citizen* (Glasgow), author of a series of articles about his visit to the Yukon entitled "The Trail of '69."
2. *Ploughman* (pp. 125-258) is Service's principal rec-

ord of his period of travel down and up the Pacific coast. References to Athol Meldrum are from *The Trail*, pp. 11-48.

3. Letter from Mr. G. C. Northwood, Manager, Personnel Data System, Canadian Imperial Bank of Commerce, Toronto, 28 Nov., 1973.
4. Mr. Northwood's letter.
5. Mr. Northwood's letter.

*Chapter 3*. The Yukon, Song and Story

1. By the Yukon Department of Travel and Information (Whitehorse).
2. Service's autobiographical account of his early years in the Yukon is in *Ploughman*, pp. 259-309, 384. The references to Meldrum and the Gold Rush are drawn from *The Trail.*
3. *Songs of a Sourdough* (1907) pp. 51-55.
4. *Ibid.*, p. 56.
5. Clipping from *The Whitehorse Star*, 26 May, 1969: in a letter by Dr. Morris Zaslow, 10 July, 1969.
6. "See Dawson City," a pamphlet issued by the Yukon Dept. of Travel and Information [1973].
7. *Ploughman*, p. 306.
8. *The Trail*, p. 48.
9. *Ibid.*, pp. 92-3.
10. Mr. Northwood's letter, 28 Nov., 1973.
11. *The New York Times Film Reviews (1913-1931)*, p. 433 (21 March, 1928).
12. *Ploughman*, 79-81, 83.

*Chapter 4*. Farewell to the North

1. This chapter is based on Service's autobiographical account in *Ploughman*, pp. 313-394 and the continuation in *Harper of Heaven* (1948), pp. 1-34.
2. *The New York Times Film Reviews (1913-1931)*, p. 433, 21 March, 1928.
3. Mr. J. L. Davies gave the author a map of this trip.
4. *The Trail*, p. 209.
5. *Rhymes of a Rolling Stone* (Briggs edition, 1912) pp. 88-89.
6. *Ibid.*, pp. 133-36.
7. At this point Service's second autobiographical volume, *Harper of Heaven*, begins.

*Chapter 5.* The Literary World
1. This chapter is mainly devoted to a study of Service's novel *The Pretender* (1914) and its main character, James Madden. References to Service's account of his own first years in Paris are based on *Harper of Heaven,* pp. 35-51. The quotation is from *Harper,* p. 48.
2. *The Pretender,* pp. 161-62 and 231.
3. *Harper,* pp. 48-49.
4. *Ballads of a Bohemian* (1921), p. 148.
5. Letters from Mrs. E. G. Berry of Winnipeg, 15 Jan., 1974; also letters from Mr. L. E. Bartz, Art Registrar, Glenbow-Alberta Institute, Calgary, 21 March, 1974; and *150 Years of Art in Manitoba* (Winnipeg Art Gallery, 1970).
6. Mrs. Service's letter. 15 July, 1975.
7. *Harper,* pp. 43-46, 60-61, 96-97, 181-85.
8. *The Trail,* pp. 208-213.
9. *The New York Times Film Reviews (1939-1948),* pp. 1867-68, 22 May, 1942; *Harper,* pp. 17, 411-417.
10. *Pretender,* pp. 91-100.
11. *Ibid.,* p. 251.
12. *Harper,* p. 44.
13. [See p. 18.]

*Chapter 6.* Parisian Idyll, The Great War, and Hollywood
1. *Harper,* pp. 51-55.
2. Mrs. Service's letter, 4 Dec., 1963.
3. This chapter is based upon Service's autobiographical account of his Parisian years 1913-1922 in *Harper,* pp. 51-138, with supplemental references to Service's observations, descriptions and fictions in *The Pretender* (1914), *Rhymes of a Red Cross Man* (1916), *Ballads of a Bohemian* (1921), and *The Poisoned Paradise* (1922).
4. *Harper,* pp. 52-61.
5. *Pretender,* p. 103.
6. *Ibid.,* p. 109.
7. *Ibid.,* p. 302.
8. *Ibid.,* pp. 258-59.
9. *Ibid.,* p. 262.
10. *Ibid.,* pp. 59-71.

11. *Harper,* pp. 73-94.
12. *Red Cross Man,* pp. 156-57.
13. *Ploughman,* p. 344.
14. *Ballads of a Bohemian,* pp. 197-98.
15. *Ibid.,* pp. 70-72.
16. The Viking Press (N.Y., 1958), pp. 51-73.
17. *The New York Times Film Reviews (1913-1931),* p. 200, 9 June, 1924.
18. *Ibid.,* p. 200.
19. *Harper,* pp. 170-75.
20. Mrs. Service's letter, 15 July, 1975.
21. *The Poisoned Paradise,* p. 343.
22. *Ibid.,* p. 95.
23. *The New York Times Film Reviews (1913-1931),* p. 207, 11 [?] August, 1924.

*Chapter 7.* Tales of Evil in Paradise
 1. *Harper,* p. 138.
 2. *Ibid.,* pp. 108-143.
 3. *Ibid.,* p. 159.
 4. *Roughneck,* p. 27.
 5. *Ibid.,* p. 149.
 6. *The New York Times Film Reviews (1913-1931),* p. 222, 3 Dec., 1924.
 7. *Why Not Grow Young?,* p. 57.
 8. *Harper,* pp. 136-159.
 9. *Ibid.,* p. 158.
10. *Ibid.,* p. 158.
11. *House of Fear,* p. 101.
12. *Harper,* pp. 193-94.

*Chapter 8.* New Adventures
 1. Quotation from *Why Not Grow Young?* (1928). Geoffrey T. Hellman reports that Service refused Frank Dodd's request for an autobiography [about 1941] but sent the completed *Ploughman of the Moon* to the publisher late in 1944. See Hellman's profile of Service, "Whooping It Up," in the March 30th and April 6th, 1946 issues of *The New Yorker.*
 2. Mrs. Service's letter, May 1974.
 3. *Harper,* pp. 203-287.
 4. *Ibid.,* pp. 287-383.
 5. *Ibid.,* pp. 384-401.
 6. *The Star Weekly,* 17 Aug., 1940.

7. Clipping from *The Free Press*, London, Ontario, 11 Sept., 1940.
8. *Harper*, pp. 402-425.
9. *The New York Times Film Reviews (1939-1948)*, pp. 1867-68, 22 May, 1942.
10. *Harper*, pp. 411-17.
11. Public Archives of Canada, mss. M6-30 D124, Vol. 1.

*Chapter 9*. Songs in Autumn
1. Mrs. Service's letter, 8 June, 1974.
2. Since each of the five volumes bound together under the title of *More Collected Verse* has a separate numbering of pages, the following abbreviations will be used in the text of this chapter: MCV for the whole volume, SL for *Songs of a Sun-Lover;* RR for *Rhymes of A Roughneck;* LLB for *Lyrics of a Lowbrow;* Reb. for *Rhymes of a Rebel;* SS for *Songs For My Supper.*
3. Abbreviations: LCV for *Later Collected Verse;* Codg. for *Carols of an Old Codger;* Rags for *Rhymes For My Rags;* CC for *Cosmic Carols.*

**Books by Robert W. Service**
(First publication only)

*Songs of a Sourdough*
  Toronto: William Briggs, 1907
  London: T. Fisher Unwin, 1907
*The Spell of the Yukon*
  [U.S.A. title for *Songs of a Sourdough*]
  New York: Barse and Hopkins [1907]
  Philadelphia: E. Stern and Co., 1907
*Ballads of a Cheechako*
  Toronto: William Briggs, 1909
  New York: Barse and Hopkins [1909]
  Philadelphia: E. Stern and Co., 1909
*The Trail of Ninety-Eight, A Northland Romance*
  [title page has '98]
  Toronto: William Briggs, 1910
  New York: Dodd, Mead, 1910
*Rhymes of a Rolling Stone*
  Toronto: William Briggs, 1912
  New York: Dodd, Mead, 1912
  London: T. Fisher Unwin, 1913
*The Pretender, A Story of the Latin Quarter*
  New York: Dodd, Mead, 1914
  London: T. Fisher Unwin, 1915
*Rhymes of a Red Cross Man*
  Toronto: William Briggs, 1916
  New York: Barse and Hopkins, 1916
  London: T. Fisher Unwin, 1916
*Ballads of a Bohemian*
  Toronto: G. J. McLeod [1921]
  New York: Barse and Hopkins [1921]
  London: T. Fisher Unwin, 1921
*The Poisoned Paradise. A Romance of Monte Carlo*
  New York: Dodd, Mead, 1922
  London: T. Fisher Unwin, 1922
*The Roughneck* [A Tale of Tahiti]
  New York: Barse and Hopkins, 1923
*The Master of the Microbe. A Fantastic Romance*
  New York: Barse and Hopkins [1926]
  London: T. Fisher Unwin, 1926
*The House of Fear. A Novel*
  New York: Dodd, Mead, 1927
  London: T. Fisher Unwin, 1927

*Why Not Grow Young? or, Living for Longevity*
    New York: Barse and Co., [1928]
    London: Ernest Benn, 1928
*The Collected Verse of Robert Service*
    London: Ernest Benn [1930]
*The Complete Poems of Robert Service*
    New York: Dodd, Mead, 1933
*Twenty Bath-Tub Ballads*
    London: Francis, Day and Hunter, 1939
*Bar-Room Ballads. A Book of Verse*
    New York: Dodd, Mead, 1940
    London: Ernest Benn, 1940
*Ploughman of the Moon. An Adventure Into Memory*
    New York: Dodd, Mead, 1945
    London: Ernest Benn, 1946
*Harper of Heaven. A Record of Radiant Living*
    New York: Dodd, Mead, 1948
    London: Ernest Benn, 1948
*Songs of a Sun-Lover. A Book of Light Verse*
    New York: Dodd, Mead, 1949
    London: Ernest Benn. 1949
*Rhymes of a Roughneck. A Book of Verse*
    New York: Dodd, Mead, 1950
    London: Ernest Benn, 1950
*Lyrics of a Lowbrow. A Book of Verse*
    New York: Dodd, Mead, 1951
    London: Ernest Benn, 1951
*Rhymes of a Rebel. A Book of Verse*
    New York: Dodd, Mead, 1952
    London: Ernest Benn, 1952
*Songs For My Supper. Verse*
    New York: Dodd, Mead, 1953
    London: Ernest Benn, 1953
*Carols of an Old Codger. Verse*
    New York: Dodd, Mead, 1954
    London: Ernest Benn, 1954
*More Collected Verse*
    New York: Dodd, Mead, 1955
    London: Ernest Benn, 1955
*Rhymes For My Rags*
    New York: Dodd, Mead, 1956
    London: Ernest Benn, 1956
*Later Collected Verse*
    New York: Dodd, Mead, 1960